W9-BMC-835

GARDEN POOLS AND FISHPONDS

RON WARRING

Garden Pools and Fishponds

STANLEY PAUL / LONDON

STANLEY PAUL & CO LTD
178–202 Great Portland Street, London W1

AN IMPRINT OF THE HUTCHINSON GROUP

London Melbourne Sydney Auckland
Wellington Johannesburg Cape Town
and agencies throughout the world

First published 1971

*This book has been set in Imprint type, printed in Great Britain
on antique wove paper by Anchor Press, and
bound by Wm. Brendon, both of Tiptree, Essex*

ISBN 0 09 107560 2

CONTENTS

AUTHOR'S NOTE

The writer is particularly grateful to Bill Heritage who spent a lot of time and trouble vetting the manuscript of this book and suggesting a number of amendments and additions to the original work. It is a very much better book as a consequence and, it is hoped, as up to date as possible. Thanks are also due to the various specialist companies mentioned for permission to use their listings of plants and various illustrations.

R.H.W.

1

Garden Pools and Fishponds

A garden pool should be considered as a feature of a garden—not a separate entity—and planned accordingly. It can be formal or informal—presenting an artificially created water scene, or one which blends into natural surroundings and looks part of nature. A formal pool, for example, could be inset in a patio, or form the centrepiece of a paved garden area. An informal pool in a small garden would more likely be located in a corner, backed by a rock garden built around a waterfall. The approach in such a case is quite different—irregular shapes and the extensive use of natural materials for building up the scene, so that the pool becomes part of a landscaped whole.

There are so many possibilities—and decisions to make— before embarking on the construction of garden pools that they are best dealt with under separate headings.

Flowers or Fish?

A garden pool can be a home for many beautiful flowering plants— water lilies, for example, which are too well known to need further description. Plant life will be more generally visible than fish during the summer months, and so many people plan a garden pool primarily from the plant side. They may then feel that fish should be excluded, because of the possible damage they could do to more valuable plants, and the additional trouble of looking after fish. At the other extreme may be the person who wants a pool full of fish, where plant life will only hide the fish and add nothing to the attraction of the pool.

Neither extreme is, in fact, a proper approach. If a garden pool

I

is planned primarily as a home for attractive aquatic plants, the introduction of a few fish will do no harm and will not add extra work in maintenance. It will only increase the attraction of the pool. Plant and fish life together can produce a natural balance, whether the pool is formal or informal. Where the main interest is fish, then plants are still necessary in order to establish a proper balance. This is dealt with in detail in Chapter 6. No fishpond will remain healthy, and with clear water, without its quota of plant life—and a few 'scavengers' like water snails thrown in for good measure!

Formal or Informal?

A *formal* pool is one of regular geometric shape—square, rectangular or circular. Being strictly geometric it is usually finished off in a similar manner, with flagged edges—e.g. see *Fig. 1.1*. It stands on its own as a showpiece and does not need additional surroundings built up, although it lends itself to ornamentation, and particularly the installation of a fountain.

An *informal* pool is irregular in shape. To make it look more natural, edging stones (if used) are also irregularly laid and the

Fig. 1.1

Fig. 1.2

natural feature extended by blending into the background—a rock garden being the obvious choice—*Fig. 1.2* and *Fig. 1.3*.

'Backing-up' Pools

Sometimes additional, very small pools can be used for enhanced effect. *Fig. 1.4*, for example, shows a miniature water garden which may be planted in a small container such as a plastic bucket or a concrete tub, forming a collection quite separate from the main pool. It would be used mainly for plants, but could also accommodate a few small fish, and a number of such miniature water gardens could be associated with a formal pool.

With an informal pool, back-up pools would also be irregular in shape, but this time quite shallow and connected to the main pool by a pipe and filled with soil—*Fig. 1.5*. Each shallow pool would, in effect, become a bog garden, full of waterlogged soil for planting out bog plants as an additional feature—and there are many attractive plants which like growing under such conditions (see Chapter 7).

Sunken or Raised?

Normally garden pools are sunk level with the surrounding ground, regardless of their type or size. A raised pool, however, can be most attractive in many gardens, and save a lot of exca-

3

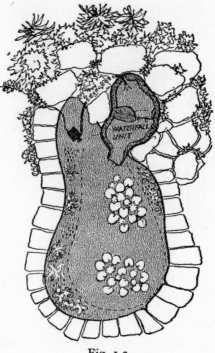

Fig. 1.3

vation. The main thing in such a case is to provide adequate support for the sides of the pool, which will be under considerable outward pressure from the weight of water filling the pool—*Fig. 1.6.*

This necessary support can itself be made a feature, expecially in the case of a formal pool, by building up a brick or stone wall surround which can, if necessary, be extended in width to form a seating area surrounding the pool. *Fig. 1.7* shows the possibilities in this direction.

Places for the Pool?

In many cases the best position for the garden pool will be dictated by the existing garden. Thus a formal pool needs to be in a 'display' position, whereas an informal pool can fill in and bring life and interest to an otherwise drab and uninteresting corner. However, the best position from the point of view of garden layout

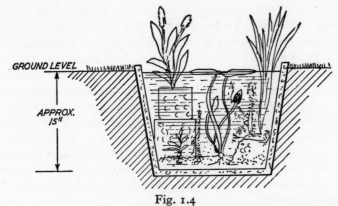

GROUND LEVEL

APPROX.
15″

Fig. 1.4

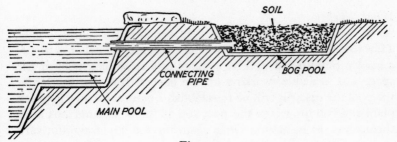

SOIL

CONNECTING
PIPE

BOG POOL

MAIN POOL

Fig. 1.5

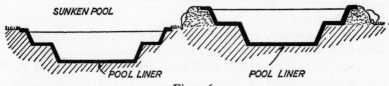

SUNKEN POOL

HALF-RAISED POOL

POOL LINER

POOL LINER

Fig. 1.6

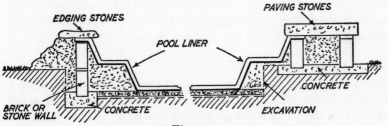

EDGING STONES

PAVING STONES

POOL LINER

BRICK OR
STONE WALL

CONCRETE

CONCRETE

EXCAVATION

Fig. 1.7

is not necessarily the best position from the point of view of the wellbeing of the pool. To become established with a good natural balance, pools need quite a bit of sunlight—so shady places under trees are to be avoided. Also they need to be in an area where they will not accumulate garden rubbish—falling leaves from trees can choke a small pool in the autumn. On the other hand, an excess of direct sunlight can make it difficult to control algae growth and maintain clear water in the pool, as well as causing excessively large variations in water temperature.

The question of site usually has to be something of a compromise, with display effect often in opposition to natural requirements. The latter will be more clearly understood after reading the remaining chapters.

What Size?

As we have already seen, a miniature water garden complete with a few fish need be no larger than bucket size. At the other extreme, a garden pond could well be as large as a swimming pool, if the space was available, working on the general rule that the larger the pool the easier it will be to establish a natural balance between plant and fish life where the pool and all its inhabitants look after themselves, as in nature. Once again there is no straightforward answer, only a compromise, although there are definite recommendations for the *minimum depth* of pools to accommodate fish—see Chapter 2.

What Materials?

The days of concrete as the only suitable construction for garden pools have largely gone. In fact, concrete is now regarded as one of the least suitable materials, both from the point of view of the considerable amount of hard work involved and the durability of the pool. Modern constructions favour the use of *lined* pools, using either flexible liner materials, or prefabricated rigid liners, such as glass fibre mouldings. Pool construction is then reduced to excavating and fitting the liner, as described in Chapter 3.

Pool Maintenance?

Provided a pool is properly proportioned and stocked with a suitable collection of aquatic plants and fish, it should settle down in a matter of a few months to a natural balance where the water will remain clear and fresh, and maintenance requirements will be a minimum. Even feeding the fish will not be necessary after the first season. And unless something really unfortunate happens—such as an outbreak of a contagious fish disease, or accidental poisoning of the water with weed killer or a garden spray—it should never be necessary to empty the pond again for 'cleaning out'. For this reason ponds do not need drain plugs, which are likely to be more than a nuisance than a help if fitted anyway.

Pool maintenance is dealt with in detail in Chapter 10 and can be reduced to simple seasonal treatment, as summarised in the table given in that chapter.

Decisions?

Most of the other questions which will arise in setting up and establishing a pool are covered in the succeeding chapters. Decisions will still have to be made—deciding on what type of pool liner to use, for example—after studying the appropriate chapter. But that is part of the enjoyment of planning a garden pool, and by studying the facts available first, mistakes can be avoided which could be disappointing and costly.

There is much more to setting up a garden pool than simply going out and buying a prefabricated pool liner and a few fish and hoping that it all works out! On the other hand, there is nothing at all difficult in establishing a properly balanced pool which will continue to remain a source of satisfaction and interest for years—all for a very modest initial outlay.

2

Pool Shapes and Proportions

A pool which is too shallow will be likely to freeze solid in winter, and the water will get too hot in summer. On the other hand, regardless of its overall size, no garden pool needs to be deeper than about 30 inches. A good general rule to work to is that the pool depth should be sufficient to provide *at least* 6 gallons of water for each square foot of surface area. Since 6 gallons of water is equal to 1 cubic foot (approximately), a suitable pool depth can be worked out on this basis.

For example, take a small rectangular pool 4 feet long by $2\frac{1}{2}$ feet wide. The surface area is $4 \times 2\frac{1}{2} = 10$ square feet, which from the rule above would require $10 \times 6 = 60$ gallons, or 10 cubic feet of water. Since the surface area is 10 square feet this would mean a depth of 1 foot, or 12 inches. This would be about right, although bearing in mind that it is a common fault to make a pool too shallow, a *minimum depth of 15 inches* would be better. This will also compensate for the fact that the pool will not be straight-sided, and may also have ledges—both reducing the actual volume of water.

The basic rule for depth can be written in more specific terms, to save unnecessary working out:

(i) pool surface area up to 60 square feet, *minimum* depth 15 inches.

(ii) pool surface area 60–80 square feet, *minimum* depth 24 inches.

(iii) pool surface area over 80 square feet, *maximum* depth 30 inches.

Few garden pools are likely to exceed 100 square feet in surface

8

area. For very large pools—say 150 square feet or more—a greater depth would probably be advisable, running to 3 to 4 feet in order to achieve a better temperature balance throughout the water.

In the case of an irregular-shaped pool the surface area can easily be estimated by 'boxing' the shape with a rectangle to give an equivalent area—see *Fig. 2.1*. The surface area then follows by multiplying together the length and width of the equivalent rectangle. From the surface area so found, a suitable depth can be decided, knowing that this will give a sufficient volume of water. The surface area can also be used later to determine the number of plants and fish the pool can support—see Chapter 6.

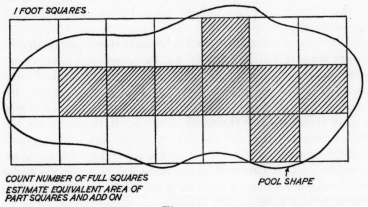

COUNT NUMBER OF FULL SQUARES
ESTIMATE EQUIVALENT AREA OF
PART SQUARES AND ADD ON

Fig. 2.1

The Pool in Cross Section

The sides of a pool should *always* be inclined, not vertical, as this will reduce the risk of ice damage. Ice, as it is formed, can 'ride up' the sides, rather than be trapped and press against them. A slope of 10 to 20 degrees is usually adequate—see *Fig. 2.2*—although this may be increased slightly in the case of a concrete pool (see Chapter 5). An excessive slope should be avoided as this will only reduce the volume of water in the pool, and offers no advantage.

There is considerable misconception as regards the depth of water required by many aquatic plants, particularly water lilies. Many water lilies, particularly those of vigorous growth, like up

9

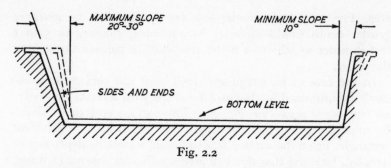

Fig. 2.2

to 18 inches of water, and will tolerate more. A depth of 24–30 inches is about the maximum they will tolerate. Thus a maximum depth of 18–24 inches is perfectly adequate for growing any species of water lily, as well as other aquatic plants normally associated with 'deep' water.

In the case of water lilies what is far more important is adequate surface area. If this is restricted the leaves will not have room to spread, stems, will bunch up and can be literally pushed out of the water as further growth develops. This is often marked after a period of a few years where the crown has developed a number of new growing parts thrusting upwards. If these do not have room to spread they will continue to grow upwards. From the result it may appear that the water lily has not got enough depth of water. In fact it means that the plant has outgrown the surface area available and needs separating and replanting in other areas where there is water surface available for development.

Other plants, which contribute to a balanced pond, are known as marginals because they naturally grow round the edges in shallow water. The majority of these are happiest with up to 3 inches of water above soil level. They will 'drown' in deeper water. Thus marginal plants will have to be carried above bottom level, and the best idea here is to shape the pool with ledges. These can run all round the pool, whether the shape is regular or irregular, lying about 9–12 inches below water level—*Fig. 2.3*. This will enable the marginals to be planted in separate containers which are stood around the ledges; or an edging built up on the ledge with bricks or stone slabs to hold soil into which the marginals can be planted direct.

Built-up edges to a ledge are less satisfactory since they are difficult to keep in place under the weight of soil. Also plant roots

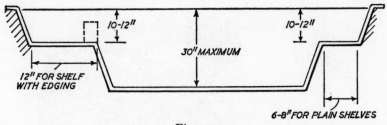

Fig. 2.3

develop throughout the extent of the ledge, intertwining and making thinning out difficult or even impossible. The same limitation applies in the case of built-in troughs in the wall section. Planting in separate containers which are stood on a ledge is the modern method, and generally to be preferred.

The required cross section of a pool, of any size or shape, is thus more or less completely defined by *Fig. 2.3*, allowing a shelf width of 6 to 8 inches to accommodate plant holders; or a shelf width of 12 inches if made with a built-up edge and filled with soil. In the case of pools fitted with liners (Chapter 3), the shelf edges would be added after the liner has been fitted and the pool filled with water.

What Size is Best?
There is no real answer to what is the 'best' size of garden pool, except to say 'the bigger the better'. Small pools, once established, rapidly tend to become overgrown with aquatic plants. Fish also grow in size, demanding more water for comfortable living. What may appear a nicely balanced pool after the first year may well end up completely overcrowded and overstocked in a few more years.

Most people tend to favour smaller sizes of pools, primarily because they are so much cheaper initially; and partly because the average garden does not have sufficient space to accommodate a large pool without it becoming out of proportion with its surroundings. A pool needs to become part of a garden, blending in with its surroundings, or planned to add interest to an otherwise dull area. The total area it occupies may well be twice as much as that of the surface area of the pool—e.g. see *Figs. 2.4 and 2.5*.

Plant life can, of course, be kept in check by weeding out,

Fig. 2.4

but this often results in considerable disturbance of the whole pool. Even if initially planted in containers, roots will spread and intertwine with others forming almost a solid 'floor' on a shelf or pool bottom. Part of the enjoyment of the pool may also be lost by plants hiding nearly all the water area, so that the fish are no longer visible, except occasionally. All these factors are in favour of choosing the largest pool size practical to start with.

Fig. 2.5

How Many Gallons?

The actual water capacity of a pool is largely an academic figure, although strictly speaking it is the major factor which governs the number of fish a pool can support. Following the general rules given for pool depth, the livestock capacity of a pool can be worked out merely on the surface area. The basic rule here is that one-third of a square foot of water surface area should be allowed for each inch of body size of fish, which means, for example, that a 30 square foot pool would be capable of supporting 90 inches of fish body length. Put more realistically, that would mean 40 fish each 2 to 3 inches long; or 20 fish each 4 to 5 inches long, and so on. A suitable complement of plant life can be worked out on surface area on a similar basis. These two subjects are dealt with in detail in Chapter 6.

For any given size of pool the fish capacity can be increased by aerating the water, such as by incorporating a fountain or waterfall which provides recirculation of water and agitation with aerated water. In such cases an increase in population of about one third can be accommodated. However, it is seldom wise to rely on such measures as a means of keeping an overpopulated pool healthy. It is better to maintain a 'static water' population figure as a maximum, even if the pool does have a fountain and/or waterfall.

In the case of proprietary rigid pools the gallonage is often stated. This is a more suitable figure for working out a suitable plant and fish population for shapes may vary considerably, and depths may not follow recommended proportions. It also saves having to work out an equivalent surface area, in the case of irregular-shaped pools.

The gallonage figure for a home-made pool can be estimated approximately by multiplying the surface area by 6 for 15 inch deep pools; 7 for 24 inch deep pools; and 8 for 30 inch deep pools. It is not necessary to be more exact than this—e.g. see Table II.

An interesting exercise, which again is mainly of academic interest, is to work out the weight of water in a pool. A gallon of water weighs 10 pounds. A pool with a surface area of 100 square feet would have a gallonage of approximately $8 \times 100 = 800$, equivalent to a weight of water of nearly four tons! The engineering-minded reader may care to work out the corresponding stress on a pool liner, the maximum tensile strength of such materials being of the order of 1,000 to 2,000 pounds per square inch.*

Table I gives true conversions for gallons to cubic feet and cubic feet to gallons. Bear in mind, however, that it is surface area rather than gallonage which really counts in deciding the 'population capacity' of any pool—both for plant and fish life.

TABLE I
CUBIC FEET TO GALLONS

Cubic feet	0	1	2	3	4	5	6	7	8	9
—	—	6·2	12·5	18·7	24·9	31·1	37·4	43·6	49·8	56·0
10	62·2	68·5	74·7	81·0	87·2	93·4	100·0	106	112	118
20	125	131	137	143	149	156	162	168	174	181
30	187	193	199	206	212	218	224	230	237	243
40	249	255	262	268	274	280	287	293	299	305
50	311	318	329	330	336	343	349	355	361	368
60	374	380	386	392	399	405	411	417	429	430
70	436	442	448	455	461	467	473	480	486	492
80	498	505	511	517	523	529	536	542	548	554
90	561	567	573	579	586	592	598	604	610	617
100	623									

GALLONS TO CUBIC FEET

Gallons	10	20	30	40	50	60	70	80	90	100
Cubic feet	45·5	91	136	182	227	273	318	364	409	455

* Worked out, this will give a stress on the liner material of the order of only 80 pounds per square inch, or a safety factor of something like 12 to 25 to 1.

TABLE II APPROXIMATE GALLONAGE OF GARDEN POOLS

Minimum pool depth 15 inches

Surface area (sq. ft.)	5	10	15	20	25	30	35	40	45	50	55	60
Gallons	30	60	90	120	150	180	210	240	270	300	330	360

Minimum pool depth 24 inches

Surface area (sq. ft.)	60	65	70	75	80	85	90	95	100
Gallons	420	455	490	525	560	595	630	665	700

Maximum pool depth 30 inches

Surface area (sq. ft.)	80	90	100	110	120	130	140	150
Gallons	630	710	800	880	960	1040	1120	1200

3

Pools with Liners

The simplest and least expensive way of making a garden pool is to dig out a hole of suitable shape and then line it with a water-proof plastic sheet. Although this may seem too simple to be true at first sight, more home-made pools are produced by this method than any other and the results can be entirely satisfactory and long lasting, using plastic sheet materials specially manufactured as pool liners.

Suitable lining materials are summarised in Table III together with their leading characteristics. All are suitable for making permanent pools, with the exception of polythene. Unreinforced PVC also has limitations as regards the maximum size of liner which can be expected to give satisfactory service. There is probably little to choose between the other liner materials, although butyl rubber sheet is by far the most stretchable. This can be significant, especially when constructing an irregular-shaped pool, because the beauty of using a flexible liner is that it is simply laid out flat over the top of the excavation and automatically formed to shape by running in water. Table IV can be used as a further guide, rating liner materials under strength, stretch, durability, etc.

Polythene Liners.
It will be noticed that polythene is rated only as semi-flexible material, and bottom of the list as regards stretch. It is the one material which cannot be stretched in place by the weight of water. It has to be laid and folded in place, which calls for a slightly different technique both in preparing the excavation and fitting the liner.

The one advantage offered by polythene is that it is by far the cheapest of the liner materials. However, the strength is relatively low and the material tends to become brittle at low temperatures, or after prolonged exposure to sunlight. A pool made with such a liner can only be regarded as having a limited life, the duration of which will depend largely on how carefully the pool is constructed and the subsequent exposure it receives. Also the larger the pool the greater the risk of failure developing as there is more area which could fail, or is open to damage.

Only 500 gauge (heavy gauge) polythene is suitable for pool liners. As a general rule, a double thickness should always be used—either two separate sheets laid together or a single large sheet doubled over. Colours normally available are black and blue, the latter being the normal choice for liners. Some two-sheet pool liner packs may comprise black and blue sheets, when the blue would be laid uppermost.

Because of the strictly limited stretch and 'mouldability' of the material under the weight of water, a regular pool shape is to be preferred when using polythene liners. This should be excavated with a generous slope to the walls (about 30 degrees), and to a suitable depth (see Chapter 2). The actual size of polythene sheet material required can then be measured, using a linen tape, as shown in *Fig. 3.1*. Measure the complete surface length from

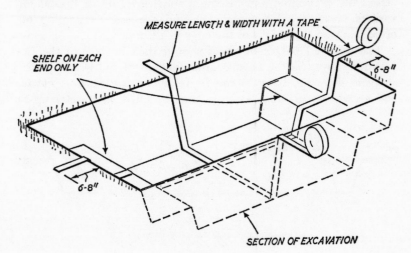

Fig. 3.1

end to end; and from side to side. Allow an extra foot on each dimension for the turned over top edges, to arrive at the final size of sheet required. If a linen tape is not available, these lengths can be determined with a length of string, subsequently measured off with a ruler.

Having arrived at the overall size of sheet required, remember that *two* sheets of this size (or one sheet of double width) must be ordered.

Alternatively, instead of actual measurement of the excavation Table V can be used to determine the proportions of a pool which can be lined by standard sizes of polythene sheet liners. Pool dimensions in this table allow for shelves.

Before attempting to lay the liner in place the excavation requires some further treatment. Remove any stones and smooth the surface of the bottom, walls and shelves as far as possible. The whole of the pool surface should then be covered with a 2-inch layer of fine sand or well sieved soil, which can be moistened as necessary to hold it in place. Additionally, some authorities recommend a final lining with layers of damp newspaper to provide an even, smooth surface on which the polythene can be laid.

It is important that the edges of the excavation be level, otherwise a varying depth of pool liner will be exposed above the water surface when filled. Level can be checked by laying a plank across the excavation and placing a spirit level on it. Repeat for various positions of the plank around the edge, trimming off or packing up the height of the edge as necessary.

The doubled polythene sheet should then be laid in the excavation, covering the bottom and sides up to the height of the shelves—*Fig. 3.2*. Corners can be folded in the form of pleats, and tucked under. The pool can then be filled with water up to

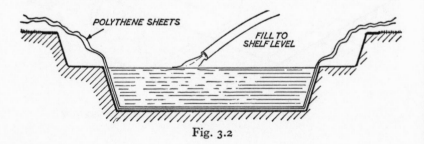

POLYTHENE SHEETS

FILL TO
SHELF LEVEL

Fig. 3.2

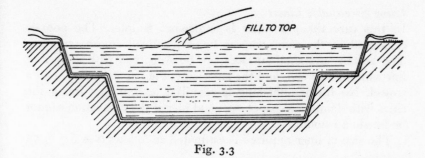

Fig. 3.3

shelf height. This will mould the liner to the bottom shape and also hold it in place whilst the sheet is folded and tucked under to complete covering the top half of the pool—*Fig. 3.3*. Never *cut notches* in the edge. Finally fill the pool up to the top, then fold surplus material flat with the surface of the ground. Trim off with scissors leaving an edge four or five inches wide. This edge can be held down flat, and completely hidden, with a layer of paving slabs or flat rocks laid right round the edge of the pool—*Fig. 3.4*. These should have a slight over-hang to hide the edge.

Polythene liners can be used with irregular-shaped pools. In this case design the outline shape to come within the rectangular dimensions of Table V and select the polythene sheet size accordingly. Laying and filling procedure is similar, except that more care will be needed in folding to minimise the number of creases and tucks. Most of the creases will disappear under the weight of the water moulding the liner to the excavation.

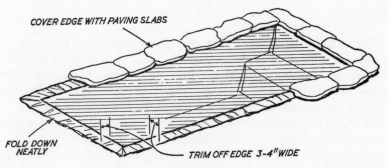

Fig. 3.4

Using Stretchable Liners

In this case the procedure is somewhat simpler. The pool is excavated in the same way as before, and all stones removed. The bottom and shelf surfaces can be smoothed with a layer of fine sand or fine soil, and the sides smoothed as necessary with a trowel. No further finishing is required, except that lining the sides with damp newspaper is a good idea if the excavation cannot be finished smooth.

The size of liner required is estimated as follows (see *Fig. 3.5*):

Length=overall length of pool plus twice the maximum depth.
Width=overall width of pool plus twice the maximum depth.

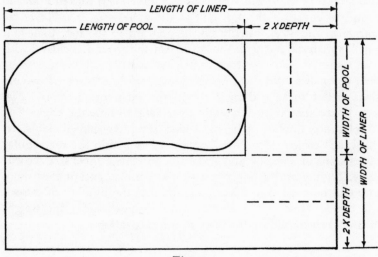

Fig. 3.5

It will be appreciated that this gives maximum economy of material with a rectangular-shaped pool. However, stretchable liners are equally suitable for irregular-shaped pools, although this may involve some waste of material since the size required is based on overall or maximum length and width dimensions— see *Fig. 3.6*. In the case of a non-rectangular pool, a kidney shape or similar will give maximum economy of material.

Laying the liner in place is very straightforward—see *Fig. 3.7*. It is simply laid out flat over the excavation with the edges weighted

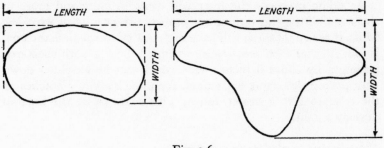

Fig. 3.6

down with bricks or paving slabs, distributing these evenly all round. Pull the liner taut and reasonably free from wrinkles with a slight sag in the middle. Commence filling the pool with water, pouring it onto the centre of the liner. As the pool fills the weight of water will drag the liner down into the excavation, partly by the material stretching and partly by the edges slipping inwards. Keep a check to see that the material edge does not pull over the edge of the excavation. If this threatens, pull it back and weight down more firmly, but *do not peg* the material down, as this will only cause it to develop a tear.

Fig. 3.7

As filling proceeds the liner will conform more and more to the shape of the excavation, but probably show a lot of wrinkles. Most, if not all, of these will have disappeared by the time the pool is full. All that then remains is to trim off the edges with scissors, leaving a lip about 6 inches wide which can be weighted down with paving slabs and flat stones. Again *do not* cut v-notches in the edge to give a neater finish. This could cause the liner to develop a split.

Stretchable Liner Materials

The above technique applies to all liner materials listed in Tables III and IV, with the exception of polythene. Some further notes on the properties of these materials are given under the separate headings following.

PVC

The PVC materials used for proprietary pool liners have been specially formulated to provide good strength and flexibility, with excellent resistance to ageing and embrittlement. They are less durable than the reinforced sheet plastics, but more economical. They are available in colours, blue and stone being the usual choice for pools, also 'overprinted' with a pebble effect. Double laminated PVC sheet can be two-coloured, e.g. stone on one side and blue on the other. In this case either side can be laid uppermost.

Reinforced PVC

These materials are much stronger and there is virtually no limit to the size of pool which can be lined. Sheets are available in almost any width required, and virtually unlimited length. If necessary sheets can be joined by welding, to produce different shapes or sizes. Colours generally available include blue, green, stone and pebble effect*. Double laminated reinforced sheet can be two-tone, one colour on each side.

All PVC materials are durable and the reinforced materials can be considered as permanent, although they can be expected to age slowly under the action of sunlight and eventually become somewhat brittle. It is impossible to give any definite figure for

* The production of 'pebble effect' colours ceased in 1970.

22

life, but a minimum of ten years can be anticipated, provided the pool liner is laid properly in the first place.

Butyl Rubber

This is a much more elastic material than the PVC liners and thus moulds more easily and regularly to awkward shapes. It would thus be preferred for lining an irregular-shaped pool, particularly if complete absence of wrinkling is required. Most PVC liners will show some wrinkling, but wrinkles should normally be absent with a butyl liner.

Butyl rubber has an indefinite life, being completely unaffected by sunlight, frost or weather. It is, however, not as strong as reinforced PVC and thus needs a little more care in handling.

In service some butyl rubber liners have shown an unexpected limitation, namely the possibility of plant and root growth passing through the material itself. This is likely to occur only when the material is extensively stretched. Thus one of the main attractions of the liner material can produce unexpected side effects. For this reason, many suppliers of pool liners have dropped butyl rubber as a material. Others may continue to supply it with the recommendation that it be laid more like polythene, rather than a true elastic material, to avoid the possibility of through growth developing.

Laying Pool Liners in Cold Weather

The elasticity or stretch of all plastic sheeting increases with increasing temperatures. It is always best to lay liners on a sunny day, when the material can first be stretched out in the sun and left to get warm and more stretchable. If used on a cold day it will help if the liner material is first warmed up by placing in a warm place for an hour or so before it is to be used—e.g. an airing cupboard, if there is room. On no account, however, should a plastic liner material be warmed up by direct heating, or be placed near a hot fire. This could result in damage to the material.

Prefabricated Liners

These are produced in both flexible and rigid forms. A flexible liner is usually fabricated from reinforced PVC panels joined together by high frequency welding. Only formal shapes are produced, designed to fit specified excavation dimensions, although the excavation does not have to follow these dimensions exactly since the material is stretchable and will re-shape itself when filled, like a straightforward stretchable liner—see *Fig. 3.8*.

Rigid liners are made from a variety of plastic materials. The cheapest types are vacuum-formed from unreinforced plastic sheet, e.g. polythene, PVC and ABS (the latter being a more expensive material, but more durable). The most durable rigid mouldings are made in glass fibre, and these are also the most expensive. Installation of all rigid mouldings is the same as that described for 'male' glass fibre mouldings described in Chapter 4.

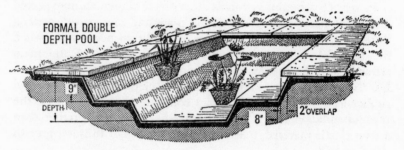

Fig. 3.8

TABLE III POOL LINER MATERIALS

Material	Elasticity	Maximum size of pool (sq. ft. surface area)	Colour(s)	Durability	Proprietary names
Polythene	semi-rigid	very small pools only	black or blue	poor	heavy gauge Polythene
Double Polythene	semi-rigid	50	black or blue	poor	heavy gauge Polythene
PVC	flexible	100	colours	good	
Laminated PVC	flexible	200	colours and two-tone	very good	'Aqualene' 'Juralene', 'Lakeliner', 'Luxipool' (three-ply)
Terylene reinforced PVC	flexible	no limit	colours and 'pebbled'	excellent	No longer produced
Nylon reinforced PVC	flexible	no limit	—	very good	—
Laminated nylon and PVC	very flexible	no limit	various	excellent	'Flexilene' 'Wavelock'
Butyl	very flexible	no limit	dark grey or black only	outstanding	Butyl

TABLE IV   PROPERTIES OF LINER MATERIALS COMPARED

Strength	Stretch	Durability	Colour choice	Lowest cost
⎧ Laminated nylon and PVC	Butyl	Butyl	Nylon/PVC Laminated PVC	Polythene
⎩ Terylene reinforced PVC*	Laminated nylon/PVC	Terylene reinforced PVC*		Double Polythene
Nylon reinforced PVC	Laminated PVC	Laminated nylon/PVC	PVC	PVC
Butyl	Terylene reinforced PVC*	Nylon reinforced PVC	Terylene reinforced PVC*	Laminated PVC
Laminated PVC	Nylon reinforced PVC	Laminated PVC	Polythene	Nylon reinforced PVC
PVC	PVC	PVC	Butyl	Terylene reinforced PVC*
Double Polythene	Polythene	Double Polythene		Butyl
Polythene	Double Polythene	Polythene		

* This material is no longer made for pool liners.

TABLE V POOL SIZES FOR STANDARD POLYTHENE SHEET LINER SIZES*

Size of liner 12 ft. wide by	Pool dimensions Length	Width	Depth	Centre deep section dimensions	Surface area sq. ft.	Capacity in gallons
3 yd.	6 ft. 6 in.	3 ft. 6 in.	15 in.	3 ft. 6 in. × 2 ft. 0 in.	22¾	100
4 yd.	9 ft. 6 in.	3 ft. 6 in.	15 in.	6 ft. 6 in. × 2 ft. 0 in.	33¼	170
5 yd.	9 ft. 0 in.	4 ft. 6 in.	18 in.	5 ft. 6 in. × 2 ft. 6 in.	40½	210
6 yd.	9 ft. 0 in.	6 ft. 0 in.	18 in.	5 ft. 6 in. × 4 ft. 0 in.	54	300

* For a rectangular-shaped pool with ledges at each end only.

4

Glass Fibre Pools

A glass fibre pool is immensely durable, but relatively expensive. Once again it is made in the form of a lining, only this time a rigid moulding which is fitted into a suitable excavation. It has the further advantage that it can be made in virtually any shape—and size, if cost is not important—and it can be self coloured.

Glass fibre pools can be bought as ready-made mouldings, or made from scratch using glass fibre mat and polyester resin. Proprietary mouldings are produced in both formal and irregular shapes, although the latter predominate, and in a range of sizes from about 4 feet by 2½ feet up to 12 feet by 5 feet. Cost normally works out roughly at 10s. to 15s. (£0·50–£0·75) per square foot or equivalent rectangular area, varying slightly with the shape. These prefabricated mouldings are usually finished in colour— light blue, light green or natural stone being common options.

Home-made glass fibre pools can be produced either as 'female or 'male' mouldings. In the former case the site is excavated to the required size and shape of the pool and the glass fibre laminations laid up in place, the dug-out hole taking the place of a mould. The alternative method is to build up a suitable pool shape, inverted, and use this as a mould to produce a glass fibre laminate which, when cured, is installed in a prepared excavation in just the same manner as a prefabricated rigid liner. This is a more lengthy method, but it has the advantage that more than one pool liner can be made from the same mould, if required.

In either case the cost of the moulding can be estimated on the basis of the actual surface area involved. This can be worked out by sketching out the shape of the pool and dividing into equivalent rectangular shapes, as shown in *Fig. 4.1*. Add together all the rectangular areas, allowing also for a 3-inch-wide rim all round the top edge, to find the approximate total surface area of the liner. The quantity of glass fibre mat and resin to match* can then be worked out on the basis that *two* layers of 1½ ounce mat will be necessary. For a larger pool it would be wiser to estimate for three layers of 1½ ounce mat, to give greater rigidity.

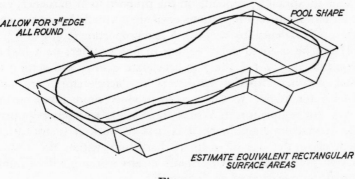

Fig. 4.1

Glass Fibre

Glass fibre mat is normally used for making mouldings because it is cheaper than woven glass fibre cloth, and also easier to drape and form to shape. It is available in different weights—typically 1 ounce per square foot, 1½ ounces per square foot and 2 ounces per square foot. The middle weight (1½ ounce mat) is the most suitable for pool liners.

Glass fibre is produced from two different types of glass—'ordinary' or soda-glass, and borosilicate glass. The latter is

* The quantity of polyester resin required to produce a satisfactory laminate can be taken as three times the weight of the glass mat. Thus for every 100 square foot of liner area, *two* layers of 1½ ounce glass fibre mat would give a glass weight of 2 × 1½ × 100=300 ounces, or 19 pounds approximately. This would require 3 × 19=57 pounds of resin. For three layers of 1½ ounce mat the amount of resin required per 100 sq. ft. of liner area would be 85 pounds, approximately. The cost of making the pool can be worked out from the quantities estimated.

29

usually called 'E' glass (developed originally for the electrical industry because of its higher resistance to moisture). 'E' type or E-grade glass is the preferred type for all mouldings which are in permanent contact with water.

Resins and Hardeners

Polyester resin cures or sets hard by chemical reaction initiated by mixing with a suitable catalyst or hardener. The setting off time, or the time taken for a resin-hardener mixture to gel and become unworkable, depends on the proportion of hardener, and the air temperature. Proportions used are normally between 1 and 4 per cent hardener (by weight). A *low* proportion (e.g. 1 or 2 per cent) can be used to delay gelling in hot weather; or a higher proportion (e.g. 4 per cent) to accelerate gelling and setting in colder weather. Special hardeners or 'accelerators' are also available for adding to the mix to produce more rapid curing at very low temperatures. Whilst these work, and generally produce satisfactory mouldings, it is best to work at temperatures which allow the use of ordinary hardeners within the 1 to 4 per cent proportion. This normally means working with a minimum air temperature of 50 degrees F.

Resin and matching hardener are usually supplied with corresponding measures, so that no difficulty should be experienced in getting the proportions right. Failing this, the following measures can be used:

4 level teaspoons of hardener = 3% hardener when added to 1 lb of resin

5 millilitres (measuring jar) = 1% hardener added to 1 lb of resin.

Moisture or dampness are the enemies of cold-setting resins. In a damp atmosphere the resin may gel, but not harden off properly. Laminates should, therefore, only be made in a dry atmosphere. Again there are additives available for producing setting in damp conditions, but these do not always work properly. It is far better to establish the proper conditions *for* working—a warm, dry atmosphere.

Fillers

Fillers are available to bulk and add through colour to glass fibre laminates. Their use is not recommended for moulded pool liners.

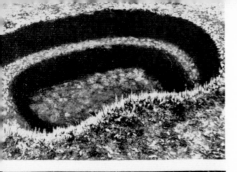

MAKING AN INFORMAL SHAPED POOL

Stage one. *The completed excavation. The shelf runs around three-quarters of the perimeter of the pool. All sharp stones should be removed from the excavation, and the surface made good by the application of a layer of sifted soil or sand.*

Stage two. *Lay the liner over the excavation, positioned so that it overlaps evenly both lengthwise and widthwise. Secure it by placing a number of paving slabs or bricks on to the liner, evenly distributed all round the edge.*

Stage three. *Commence filling with water. As the pool is filling, the weight of water will gradually take the liner down into the excavation, partly by stretching it and partly by moving the edges inwards across the ground surface. Wrinkles will appear at this stage, but will largely disappear when the pool is full.*

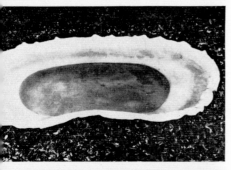

Stage four. *When the pool is full, the surplus materials should be trimmed off to leave a flap all round.*

Stage five. *The pool can then be edged with crazy paving, flat stones or rocks.*

SETTING UP A RIGID GLASS FIBRE POOL

1. *Excavation of the site; in this case a corner of a small garden.*
2. *Smoothing and preparing the bottom to take the glass fibre liner.*
3. *Setting the liner in place, checking that it is properly supported.*
4. *Filling in around the liner, consolidating to provide support.*
5. *Covering the edge with rocks, building up into a rock garden.*
6. *Plants are added in planting containers.*
7. *The completed pool and rock garden—after only five hours' work!*

Photographs by courtesy of the Minster Water Gardens

Large formal pools can take fairly massive ornamentation and form a major feature of the garden.

Straightforward treatment of a formal pool, quite uncluttered but incorporating paving as a feature.

Simple informal pool planned as a complete garden feature.

Small formal pool set in a lawn. Surrounding plants are normal herbaceous type.

Pigments

It is recommended that pigments be used in the final (or initial) gel coat to produce a coloured pool liner. These are normally available in paste form and are added in the proportion of 5 to 10 per cent to the resin. Different-coloured pigment pastes can be mixed to produce different colours or shades. Lighter colours are to be preferred to darker colours for pools, but not plain white which looks too much like a 'bathtub' colour.

Making a Lined Pool ('Female' Mould)

This is the simplest method and one which can be tackled by anyone with some previous experience of making glass fibre laminates. Since it involves making the laminate outdoors, on the site, it should, however, only be tackled in warm, dry weather as a low temperature, or dampness, will not allow polyester resin to cure properly.

The main job is digging out the ground to the shape and size of the pool required, following the general recommendations for proportions given in Chapter 2. An irregular shape is generally to be preferred with a glass fibre pool, to avoid a 'bathtub' appearance. This will also avoid sharp corners, which cannot be produced satisfactorily in glass fibre. Sides should slope quite generously and the edges of ledges, and the joint between sides and bottom, should be generously rounded (again to avoid sharp corners). It is also important to compact and finish all the surfaces as smooth as possible, removing any stones or other sharp projections. Finally make sure that the edges of the pool are quite level. Use a plank and a spirit level to check—*Fig. 4.2*.

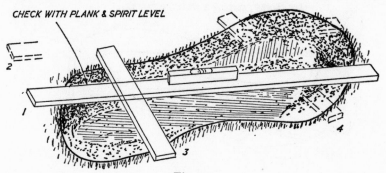

CHECK WITH PLANK & SPIRIT LEVEL

Fig. 4.2

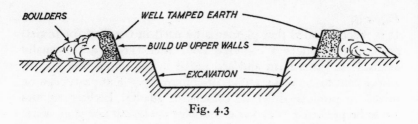

Fig. 4.3

Some considerable saving in labour is possible by making a half-raised pool. In this case the ground is only excavated to half the pool depth, or a little more, and the earth removed packed around the edge to build up to full depth—*Fig. 4.3*. This built-up edge must, however, be well tamped down and consolidated so that it will support the weight of the water in the pool. Although a rigid moulding, a glass fibre liner is flexible and can distort under the weight of water it holds, unless properly supported. Besides leaving a smaller hole to dig, a further advantage of a raised pool is that it helps keep leaves and litter from blowing along the ground into the pool.

Having prepared the excavation the surface area can be checked with a tape measure. Measure the equivalent running length and width of the equivalent rectangle, as shown in *Fig. 4.4*. This will serve as a check that enough glass mat has been bought; or give the area of glass mat required (remembering to allow for two or possibly three layers). If there is any delay between completing the excavation and starting on the laminate, cover the site with a waterproof sheet so that it will not get wet should it rain in the meantime.

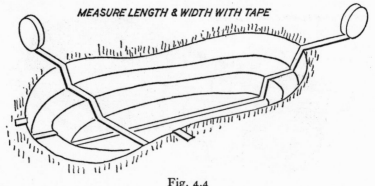

Fig. 4.4

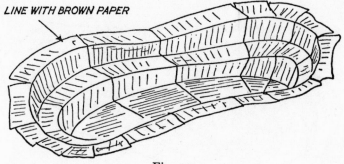

Fig. 4.5

Before the glass fibre mat can be laid in place the whole of the pool surface must be lined with something which will 'hold' the resin and stop it penetrating into the earth. Ordinary brown paper laid shiny surface up is excellent for this purpose, and is generally to be preferred to polythene sheet which is often recommended. The paper lining is simply draped and folded into place, with overlapping edges, and can be pegged in place with wire nails—*Fig. 4.5*.

The resin is then prepared by mixing with the recommended proportion of hardener. Since the resin-hardener mix has a limited pot life, only as much as can be used in that time should be prepared, bearing in mind the higher the temperature the shorter the working life of the resin. A generous coat of resin is then applied to the paper lining and a length of glass fibre mat laid in place, sufficient to run the length of the pool and overlap

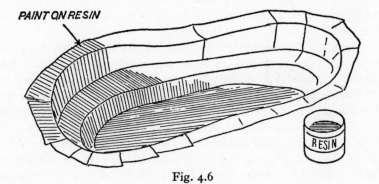

PAINT ON RESIN

RESIN

Fig. 4.6

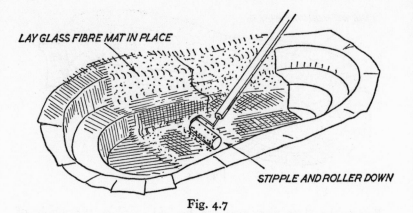

LAY GLASS FIBRE MAT IN PLACE

STIPPLE AND ROLLER DOWN

Fig. 4.7

each end—*Fig. 4.7*. Use a stiff brush to dab the mat in place and stipple the resin through, followed by a roller attached to a broom handle to squeeze out all air bubbles. These must be eliminated as they will weaken the moulding.

Other pieces of glass mat can then be torn or cut to shape (with scissors) and stippled down in place to cover the whole of the inside of the pool. Every square inch of surface area must be thoroughly wetted by resin, which is indicated by the mat changing from a white to a translucent colour, and firmed down in place.

Smooth on more resin, as necessary, to ensure that the top surface is quite wet, then lay on the next layer of glass mat. Again this must be stippled and rolled down until it is thoroughly wetted with resin and all air bubbles are excluded. Follow with a third layer of glass mat, if this is being used. The next layer is always applied whilst the resin is still wet on the first layer, as this will give the strongest moulding.

Main points to watch are to smooth and flatten down the glass mat. All joints between different pieces of mat should overlap generously and be smoothed out, not left as ridges. A fair overlap or rim should also be formed around the edge of the pool. In an hour or so, when the resin has set off but is still not completely hard, this edge can be trimmed off neatly with scissors—*Fig. 4.8*.

The complete pool should then be covered over with a waterproof sheet to prevent it getting damp. It should be left for at least a fortnight before the pond is filled with water. It takes

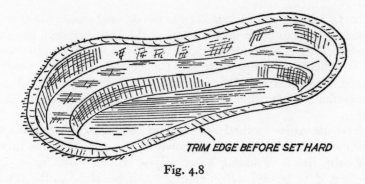

TRIM EDGE BEFORE SET HARD

Fig. 4.8

that time for the resin to set off completely and the laminate to become fully water-resistant.

Colouring Glass Fibre Pools
Plain glass fibre mouldings have an unattractive semi-translucent appearance and are best coloured. This can be done immediately after completing the lay-up of the glass mat by applying a final coat of resin which has been pigmented. This means making up a separate resin-hardener mix for the final coating, to which has been added and mixed in a suitable pigment. Suppliers of polyester resin and hardener normally offer a range of pigments in various colours and recommended proportions for their use.

Pool Mouldings from 'Male' Moulds
Two methods of making 'male' moulds are shown in *Figs. 4.9* and

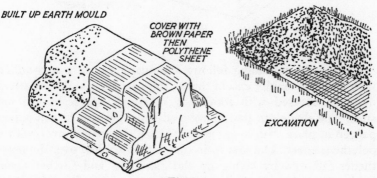

BUILT UP EARTH MOULD

COVER WITH
BROWN PAPER
THEN
POLYTHENE
SHEET

EXCAVATION

Fig. 4.9

4.10. In *Fig. 4.9* soil excavated from the site and sieved to remove stones is used to build up the shape of the liner required, but inverted. This is a simple method, but it has several limitations. It is difficult to compact the soil sufficiently to retain a proper shape. Also the shape of the liner will be different from that of the excavation, which will need further work on it to take the moulded liner.

The alternative method is to build up a suitable (inverted) shape from suitable solid objects, as shown in *Fig. 4.10*. Here the main difficulty lies in avoiding sharp edges, which would normally be formed by boxes; and in getting a suitable slope to the sides. The two methods may be combined—e.g. using boxes or similar articles to form the basic shape, then building up the mould to final shape with earth, well packed in place.

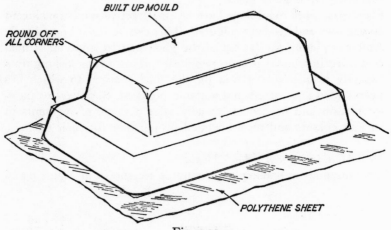

Fig. 4.10

Making the moulding follows a similar procedure to working with a female mould, except that in this case the mould or pattern must be covered with something to which the resin will not stick. The shape can first be covered with sheets of brown paper, pegged in place with long nails, and then covered all over with a polythene sheet. The first resin coat is then applied over the polythene, followed by laying up the glass mat and further resin, as necessary. The whole should then be covered with a waterproof sheet and left to set for several days before the protective cover is removed. It should then be possible to lift off the glass fibre moulding and peel off the polythene sheet. The glass fibre pool can then be fitted in its excavation, but a further week to ten days should be allowed before filling with water.

Proprietary rigid glass fibre pool mouldings are made in male moulds. In this case the moulds are permanent and finished to a smooth surface. This results in a very smooth inner surface for the pool moulding. A one-off glass fibre pool made by the method described, using a male mould, will have a smoother surface than one which is laid up in the excavation, but not as smooth and even as a proprietary moulding.

Three other important differences should also be noted with glass fibre pools made from 'male' moulds. If the pool is to be coloured, the pigment must be added to the *first* coat of resin, applied to the paper before the first layer of glass mat. The laminate must be left to set hard before it is removed from its mould, which means that the rim can only be trimmed off neatly when the laminate is quite hard. This will require the use of a hacksaw. as it is too hard to cut with scissors at this stage. Finally, of course, the moulding is a rigid liner which must be installed in a matching excavation.

Installing Rigid Liners

The same principles apply to all rigid liners, whether home-made or bought as prefabricated pools in glass fibre or other rigid plastic materials. The basic stages of installation are shown in *Fig. 4.11.*

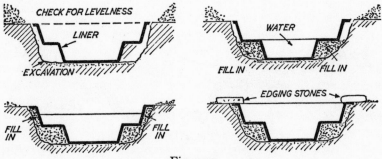

Fig. 4.11

First excavate the site, digging out a hole to the required depth but larger all round than the actual size. The bottom of the excavation should then be tamped down firmly.

The pool moulding should then be placed in position, checking that the edges line up with the edges of the excavation and that the top of the liner is level. Check this in several directions with a plank and spirit level. If necessary, insert soil under the bottom part of the liner until it is level. Then continue packing earth around the base of the liner. Make sure that the earth used does not contain sharp stones.

The pool can now be partly filled with water (provided it has 'aged' sufficiently, if home-made). Pack more earth around the sides of the pool and continue filling. Proceed in this manner until the whole of the sides of the liner are properly backed up with earth, right up to the rim. Again check the level. This will show up by the level of the water surface. If this is not true it means that part of the packing has subsided under the weight of water, distorting the liner. If bad, it may be necessary to empty the pool and re-pack the 'low' side with more earth tamped in place.

Where the liner is installed on a sloping site the procedure is similar except that the actual site area must be levelled. This is most easily done by excavating a much wider hole than necessary, digging out the higher level and building up on the low side— *Fig. 4.12*. If necessary, large stones or rocks can be used to hold back loose earth at the change of levels. A similar precaution can be adopted in the case of half raised pools, i.e. supporting the built-up earth with rocks, or even a complete walled surround in bricks or stone—see Chapter 1.

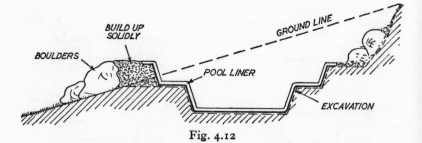

Fig. 4.12

Proprietary Glass Fibre Mouldings

Proprietary glass fibre pools are available in a very wide range of shapes and sizes. Nearly all are of informal or irregular shape, although formal shapes can also be obtained. Suppliers of such pools normally also supply matched collections of aquatic plants and fancy fish to suit the sizes of the various pools they make, which can eliminate the necessity of working these out from scratch.

A recent development is the introduction of sectional pools in glass fibre. These comprise sectional units of various shapes which can be fitted together in various combinations to produce pools of varying shapes and sizes—see *Fig. 4.13*. This means that a suitable shape can be worked out to follow garden contours; or even that the pool can be extended at a later date by the addition of further sections. The one objection to this system is the introduction of joints or seams in a rigid liner, which could be a source of leakage. However, in the event of leakage developing, such a pool could be made fully watertight by fitting with a flexible liner.

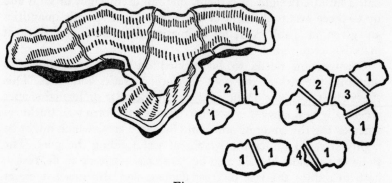

Fig. 4.13

5

Concrete Pools

The construction of a concrete pool is something of a major project. It needs to be a large pool to justify the use of concrete, when the work involved will be considerable and the amount of concrete required surprising. As a rough guide, for example, every 10 square feet of pond surface area will require at least half a hundredweight of cement, one hundredweight of sand and up to three hundredweight of aggregate. More specific quantities are given in Table VII, for estimating the actual quantities of materials required.

Construction needs to be tackled on the correct lines, to minimise the risk of the pool developing cracks and leaks. This starts right with the shape of the pool. Regular or formal shapes are usually best since it is easier to ensure a uniform wall thickness when laying the concrete and avoid localised areas which might be highly stressed under the weight of water filling the pool. The slope of the sides should also be generous—at least 20 degrees— both to reduce the risk of frost damage and also make it easier to build the walls without extensive use of shuttering to hold the wet concrete in place. Pool depth should follow the general recommendations of Chapter 2, with 30 inches the maximum required, regardless of the size of the pool, unless exceptionally large.

A plain rectangular shape with straight or sloping bottom (*Fig. 5.1*) would appear the simplest shape, involving the minimum of concrete working, but it has definite limitations. It provides no base for marginal plants (although these could be supported in containers or on bricks or rocks), and the height of the walls will

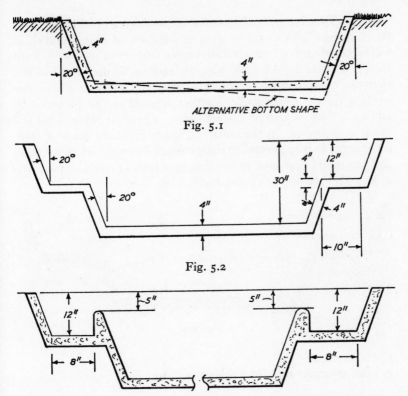

ALTERNATIVE BOTTOM SHAPE

Fig. 5.1

Fig. 5.2

Fig. 5.3

almost certainly call for the use of shuttering to keep the wet concrete in place until it has set. A shape with built-in ledges is better (*Fig. 5.2*), although unless ledges are incorporated on the sides as well as the ends, shuttering may still have to be used for the side walls.

A further variation is shown in *Fig. 5.3* where the ledges incorporate inner walls, formed in concrete. This provides a trough which can be filled with soil to take marginal plants. The construction in this case is more complicated and is best not tackled by anyone who has no previous experience of concrete work.

Preparing the Site
The site is prepared by digging out to the shape and depth required, then lining with hardcore which is tamped well down—

Fig. 5.4. This is essential in order to produce a rigid backing for the concrete. The hardcore used can consist of coarse gravel, or mixtures of gravel with small stones and clinkers. The walls should also be lined in this way, at least up to the height of the shelves. Well tamped earth will generally provide a suitable backing for the upper walls. Further support can be provided by adding a layer or two of chicken wire, pegged in place. This will become embedded in the concrete, when laid, and act as a reinforcement. It is important in such cases, however, that all the wire, and any metal pegs used to position it, is fully covered by concrete, as any exposed wire will eventually rust.

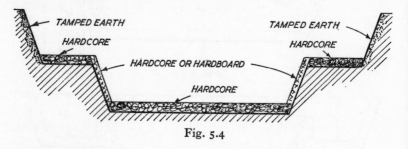

Fig. 5.4

Concrete Mixes
A basic concrete mix for pools consists of:

1 part cement
2 parts 'building' sand
5 parts crushed aggregate (1 inch sieve size)
waterproofing powder—$2\frac{1}{2}$ pounds per hundredweight of *cement* used in the mix.

The waterproofing powder is an addition to ordinary concrete mixes, so if bagged ready-mixed concrete is bought instead of the separate constituents it should be added in the proportion of $\frac{1}{2}$ pound per hundredweight of 'ready mix' and stirred in thoroughly whilst the mixture is still dry.

For convenience, the concrete should be mixed adjacent to the site. A large sheet of polythene and a 4 foot square of hardboard can be used to protect the ground, as shown in *Fig. 5.5.* The dry mix is piled up in the form of a 'mountain', hollowed out in the centre with a spade, into which water is poured. The dry solids are then turned over with the spade to mix with water, adding

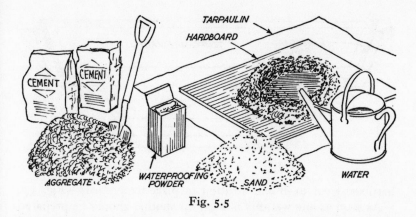

Fig. 5.5

further water from time to time as necessary to produce a firm pasty mixture of even consistency.

The wet mixture is then shovelled into the bottom of the excavation and levelled out roughly with the spade. Final levelling off is then done with a large flat trowel, aiming at achieving a smooth, even surface. Enough concrete must be laid in place to produce a final thickness of 4 inches all over. If necessary, this can be checked using a marked length of dowel as a probe, filling in the hole left by the dowel by pressure with the trowel on the wet concrete.

The sides are usually most easily formed by piling an excess of concrete mix on the shelves, then carrying this onto the walls with the trowel. Again a 4-inch thickness overall is required—*Fig. 5.6*. If a nice stiff mix is used—not too much water—it should be possible to form the sides without having to use shuttering to hold them in place until set. If the concrete does show signs of sagging or falling away, sides can be supported by sheets of

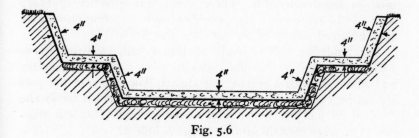

Fig. 5.6

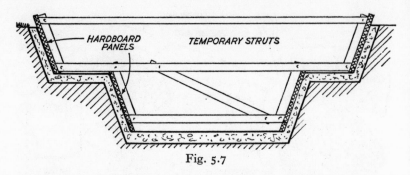

Fig. 5.7

hardboard cut to fit and strutted in place temporarily—*Fig. 5.7*.

As soon as one wet mix is used up another should be prepared and the work continued. The whole job should be completed in one session, if possible, so that 'wet' concrete is not joined to 'dry' concrete. This means that adequate material should be on hand to start with—see Table VII.

Concrete can take from one to two days, to a week, to set hard, depending on the weather. As soon as the pool has set hard enough to work on it must be given a *rendering coat* all over to a thickness of about one inch. A different cement mix is used for this, comprising:

1 part cement
3 parts sharp sand
waterproofing powder—5 pounds per hundredweight of *cement* used.

Quantities required for the rendering mix can be estimated from the fact that one hundredweight of *cement* will make enough rendering mix to cover 40 square feet to a thickness of 1 inch. In other worlds, divide the *total surface area* of the pool by 40. This will give the amount of cement required for the rendering mix, in hundredweights. Three times this quantity of sharp sand will be required; and 5 pounds of waterproofing powder for each hundred weight of cement—see also Table VI.

The rendering mix is made up into a stiff, consistent paste with water—just as for the concrete mix—and applied evenly and smoothly with a rectangular trowel. Top edges of the pool should be checked for level (with a plank and spirit level) and finished off just below the level of the ground. This will allow turf to be taken over the concrete edge to hide it.

Conditioning the Concrete Pool

Fresh concrete contains free lime which will enter into solution and poison the water as far as plant and fish life are concerned when first filled. To condition the pond, it should be thus filled and left to stand for several weeks. By this time any free lime will have been leached out, when the pond can be pumped dry and refilled with fresh water, ready for stocking up.

Fortunately there is a quicker way of 'conditioning' a concrete pool. Sealing compounds are available which can be painted onto the surface of the concrete which not only neutralise the lime but react with it to produce a form of internal glazing, thus improving the water resistance of the concrete. Ponds can be filled and stocked within a day or so of sealing.

Actually there are two types of sealing compounds—those which neutralise the lime and impart an internal glaze, as described above, and those which provide a covering 'skin' effectively isolating the concrete surface from contact with water. Neutralising and 'glazing' compounds are probably best for new concrete pools, but are quite ineffective on old concrete (because there is no free lime with which they can react). Sealing compounds which form a 'skin' coating are equally effective on both new and old coating, although in the case of new concrete must be preceded with a coat of special primer to neutralise any lime present. They also have the advantage that they can be produced in colours. Their main limitations are that they will only adhere to clean *dry* concrete, and being plastic compounds will not harden properly in very cold weather.

Typical recommendations and quantities required are summarised in Table VIII.

Only sealers specifically compounded for concrete pools should be used. Other types of chemical treatment which may be advocated for 'sealing' concrete, or other types of concrete paint, should not be used on pools intended to take plant and fish life, unless specifically known to be suitable. For example, polyester resin (plain or pigmented) could be used as a paint to provide a waterproof 'skin' coating.

Repairs to Concrete Pools

Despite their apparent ruggedness, concrete ponds can develop cracks or leaks, even when carefully constructed. This can be due to frost damage, or subsidence or other cause over stressing parts of the concrete which subsequently crack. Treatment then requires pumping out the pond dry and cleaning it, so that the damaged area may be repaired. Treatment should never be attempted by partly emptying the pool to expose a crack, as whatever material is used for repair, the risk of poisoning the remaining water is very high.

It is virtually useless to attempt to repair cracks by plastering over with concrete, since new concrete will never adhere properly to old concrete. A permanent repair can only be produced by coating over with a skin-forming sealing compound; although in the case of large cracks the gap should be filled first with new concrete. An alternative repair medium is glass fibre and polyester resin—using filler for filling in cracks, followed by a 'bandage' coating of glass mat or cloth over the damaged area, applied with resin. This will only adhere properly if the concrete surface is clean and dry, and the air temperature is not less than 50 degrees F.

For simple cracks, two or three coats of skin-forming sealer should provide a permanent repair. If several cracks are suspected, it may be as well to apply two coats of sealer overall, having gone to the trouble of emptying and cleaning out the pond to start with. This can also provide some protection should further cracks develop in the course of time.

An alternative method where a concrete pool leaks very badly, or cannot be cured satisfactorily by the use of sealer, is to fit a plastic liner to the whole pool, as described in Chapter 3. This at least can be relied upon to produce a completely positive cure, and a safeguard against leakage should further cracks develop. The durability of the pool is then as good as the lasting qualities of the material chosen for the liner.

TABLE VI QUANTITIES FOR RENDERING MIX

Pool surface area (sq. ft.)*	10	20	30	40	50	60	70	80	90	100
Cement (lb) †	4·5	9	13·5	18	22·5	27	31·5	36	40·5	45
Sharp sand (lb)	14	27	40	54	68	81	95	108	122	135

* Total surface area.
† Add 5 lb of waterproofing powder per *hundredweight* of cement used, and pro rata.

TABLE VII ESTIMATION OF QUANTITIES REQUIRED

Pool surface area (sq. ft.)*	10	20	30	40	50	60	70	80	90	100
Amount of cement (lb) †	60	120	180	240	300	360	420	480	540	600

* Total surface area of pool, including bottom, sides and ledges. Corresponding quantities of the other material required are:

    TWICE this figure for sand

    FIVE TIMES this figure for crushed aggregate.

† $2\frac{1}{2}$ lb of waterproofing powder per *hundredweight* of cement used, and pro rata.

TABLE VIII QUANTITIES FOR CONCRETE SEALING COMPOUNDS

Type	Quantity	Remarks
Waterproofing Powder	$2\frac{1}{2}$ lb per hundredweight of cement used for concrete 5 lb per hundredweight of cement used for rendering	Used in original or rendering mix
Glazing treatment	Estimate on the basis that 1 lb of solid compound dissolved in water will cover and treat 30 to 35 square feet of concrete surface	Used on new concrete only
Sealing treatment	Estimate on the basis that 1 gallon of sealing liquid will cover 50 square feet of smooth concrete in good condition with two coats. A larger quantity may be required to treat rough concrete.	Can be used to to seal new pools, also old concrete, provided the surface is cleaned. Can also be used to seal and repair fine cracks in concrete.

47

6

Setting up a New Pool

A garden pool needs setting up with aquatic plants and fish in such a manner that a balance is achieved between plant and fish life. After a while a new pool should settle down and then more or less look after itself, requiring only the minimum of maintenance, unless affected by pests or disease. It will, however, normally take at least a year for a new pool to settle down to its natural balance and maintain clean, sweet water with absence of excess algae growth.

Ordinary tap water is quite suitable for filling a pool, although rainwater is probably better if it can be collected in sufficient quantity. Stock can be introduced into the pool more or less immediately after filling, if desired, although some authorities recommend letting a newly filled pool stand for a few days first for the water to 'mature'.

Ideally the pool should be planted out with aquatic plants first and left for two or three weeks to get them acclimatised before the fish are introduced. In practice this is not always possible. Fish and plants may arrive together, or the fish before the plants. It does no harm for fish to be introduced into a perfectly plain pool, provided they are fed and the plants are added within a week or so. The only disadvantage is that the fish will probably attack the plants as soon as they are added, and before they have had time to settle down. In fact the oxygenating plants, in particular, may never get a chance to settle down properly and as a consequence the pond may never achieve a proper balance. Wherever possible, therefore, always introduce plants before fish, with an interval of two to three weeks between each.

A further practical problem which can arise is that the planting season for plants is fairly limited. May to July is the usual planting season, although this will vary slightly with different species. Oxygenating plants can usually be started earlier, in March or April, and start to grow; but no aquatic plants planted after mid-September are likely to show much signs of activity until the following late spring. Furthermore plants from specialist suppliers are unlikely to be despatched 'out of season', and so a complete order may be only partially filled at one time. Table IX provides a general guide to planting seasons.

On this basis the most logical time to set up a new pool is in the spring, when planting out can be started in April or May, with other plants to follow in June, or even later. There is really no point in trying to set up a new pool later than mid-August in any one year as it will not have time to establish even partial balance before the plants start dying down for the winter, and most of the oxygenating plants will be too brittle to plant successfully.

Plant Selection
Plants can be divided into different types, some of which are 'functional' and others mainly decorative. Every pond should incorporate a selection of both types.

Foremost amongst the functional plants are the submerged *oxygenating plants*. These will grow in any depth of water and are planted on the bottom. They absorb carbon dioxide exhaled by fish and generate oxygen. All plants do this, but oxygenating plants are very active oxygen generators, as can be seen from the numerous fine bubbles forming on their leaves.

Oxygenating plants are the most important of all types to include in a garden pond. Without sufficient active oxygenating plants it will be impossible to establish a proper balance and keep the water clear.

Floating plants are also functional in that they provide shade, and in many cases food. One objection to them is that they tend to multiply rapidly during the summer months and spread out over the whole of the pond surface. Bottom-planted plants, which develop large leaves spreading out on the water surface, are probably better for shade, but again can threaten to take over the whole surface if planted in too great a profusion.

Providing shade is important, for all plants need sunshine in

49

order to thrive, which is why a pool should always be located in a reasonably sunny position. However, sunshine and bright light will encourage green algae growth in the water. Besides providing 'umbrella' shelter for fish, therefore, shading plants perform the useful function of not letting too much light and sunshine penetrate below the surface of the water.

Water lilies are, of course, prized for their decorative value, but here some caution should be observed. Water lilies vary considerably in the vigour of their growth. Only the least vigorous are suitable for growing in smaller pools. The more vigorous varieties may need plenty of water surface area, and even then can spread out over a very large area in two or three years. Failing sufficient area of water their foliage will stand right out above the surface, with leaves drooping down in an overcrowded mass. More details of the different types available are given in Chapter 7, so that it is sufficient to state here that the numbers chosen should be restricted to allow for the depth of water available.

The other pond plants can be classified broadly as *shallow marginals* and *deep marginals*. The former are planted around the ledges of the pool and form a natural 'edge' decoration—as well as partial shelter for fish liking shallow water. Deep marginals can be planted on the bottom, or near the bottom, their stems and leaves growing up through the surface. Species of each type available are numerous, the main ones suitable for pools being described in Chapter 7.

Plant selection is simplified by buying a collection of plants from a specialist supplier. The size of such collections is planned to suit various sizes of pools, and alternatives for each size are usually available at different prices.

How Many Plants?
Whilst this question could be answered in terms of water volume, surface area and water depth, the simplest way is to work to figures which have proved satisfactory in practice, according to the size of pool in terms of surface area. This is done in Table X, grouping plants under type rather than individual species. The numbers given should be more than adequate for an initial planting, although the pool may continue to look a little bare through the first season. In two or three years, however, it will have started to become overcrowded and the plants will need thinning out.

Planting Technique

All plants are invariably planted in soil. The best type of soil is turves, laid grass side down, over which can be laid further chopped turf, fibrous loam, or even garden soil (preferably a heavy soil in this case, not light soil). Avoid using sand, leaf mould, peat or any type of manure. All are bad for the water.

Quite recently special aquatic plant fertilisers have been developed. These are based on calcium orthophosphate enclosed in perforated sachets, giving a slow release time. Embedded in the soil alongside plants they encourage rapid root development and root growth and are most effective in action.

The choice lays between planting in separate containers, or in soil laid directly on the pool bottom and shelves. The former is the modern method and generally accepted as the best technique.

Suitable containers are produced specifically for the purpose, and are available from most specialist suppliers. They comprise simple plastic 'baskets' with perforated sides, usually square in section, but in different sizes and depths—e.g. see *Fig. 6.1*. Similar plastic containers may be found in department stores, e.g. as flowerpot holders, and will do equally well if they have perforated sides and are made of plastic.

The *depth* of container is selected according to the depth of soil required for the particular type of plant concerned—e.g. see Table XI. The top size is determined by the size of plant, or how many plants are to be planted in a single container. Table XII can be used as a guide here.

Containers should normally be lined with turf, grass side out, and then filled with soil as necessary. Plants are then firmly planted in this soil. The general rule for planting is that the crown of the plant should come just above soil level, with the roots well spread out. Avoid burying the crown, as this can cause the plant

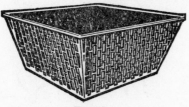

Fig. 6.1

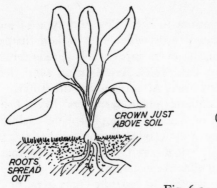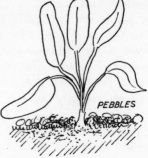

CROWN JUST
ABOVE SOIL

PEBBLES

ROOTS
SPREAD
OUT

Fig. 6.2

to rot. *Fig. 6.2* shows correct and incorrect methods of planting.

Water lilies need particular care in planting. Before planting all old or damaged leaves should be removed and the roots trimmed right back, as shown in *Fig. 6.3*. As bought, roots may be partially trimmed and so need cutting back further. Planting should then be done vertically, except in the case of certain tuberous rooted varieties which need to be planted horizontally with the crown just above soil level—*Fig. 6.4*. Firm planting is essential, as there will be a strong tendency for the lily to float upwards once immersed. Small rocks, coarse gravel, or stones on the top of the container, or surrounding the lily if planted directly in soil, will help hold it in position until the root growth becomes established.

In the case where a plant has no apparent crown or root, such as with oxygenating plants, the bottom end of the stem is simply

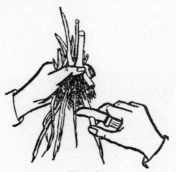

Fig. 6.3

ROOTS TRIMMED BACK

TUBER PLANTED HORIZONTALLY

Fig. 6.4

pushed into a hole made in the soil and the soil then firmed around it to hold it in place.

After planting it is always a good idea to add a layer of pebbles or coarse gravel over the top of the soil. This will not only assist in holding the plant in place by preventing soil getting washed away, but will generally improve the appearance of the 'ground' when the container is placed in position in the pool. The same treatment can also be applied to shelves fitted with edges and filled with soil. *Fig. 6.5* shows a typical planting layout embracing marginals, oxygenating plants, floating plants, deep marginals and water lilies.

Plants First
Assuming that the best arrangement is possible—planting out the plants first—the water will almost certainly go green or brown due to the formation of algae. This is not harmful and most of the green should disappear in a few weeks, once the plants get properly established and some surface shade is formed by

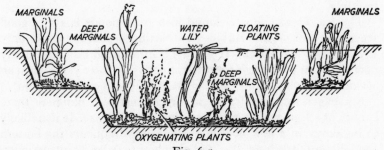
Fig. 6.5

floating leaves. Fish can still be introduced at the 'green water' stage. It will not harm them, and many fish take algae as food. If for any reason the fish have to be introduced before the plants the water will tend to get even greener, but again will clear in time as plants become settled in.

After planting the water will also be quite murky, due to disturbed soil being carried up in suspension. This should quickly settle, although finer particles or soil may remain suspended for some considerable time. Again this is not harmful, but every effort should be made when planting, or lowering containers into position, not to disturb the water excessively and distribute soil through the water.

Fig. 6.6

Scavengers

Water snails (*Fig. 6.6*) should be introduced as soon as the pool is first set up (whether with plants or fish). They are scavengers, feeding on algae and waste matter. One snail per square foot of water surface area is a good rule for numbers in a new pool. Not all may survive the initial weeks, but the remainder will multiply.

The fresh water mussel found in natural ponds is also a good scavenger, but seldom thrives in an artificial pool for it can only live on a muddy bottom. It will die if introduced into almost any new pool, but could be introduced after two or three years when an accumulation of 'natural' soil has been built up on the bottom.

Scavenger fish are also usually recommended, but here there is only one type which is really suitable—the *tench*. It is unlikely to be happy in a new pool because it only frequents the bottom and will find little food. It is probably best to delay its introduction

54

until the second season, when one tench could be introduced per 20 square foot of pool surface area.

Contrary to 'traditional' advice, a special scavenger fish is not essential in any pond. Goldfish and shubunkins themselves are effective scavengers. If scavengers are included, then one type to avoid is the catfish as this is a predator which can grow to a large size at the expense of other inhabitants of the pool.

Stocking with Fish

The allowance of 3 inches of fish body length per square foot of pool area can be adopted for deciding the maximum number of fish, of different types and sizes, which it is safe to introduce into the pool. In general it is probably best to work to a somewhat lower figure to allow for the fact that it will take time for the pool to become properly established, and to allow for subsequent growth and multiplication by natural breeding. Fish can normally be introduced into a pool any time between April and mid-October.

The choice of fish is relatively open. Fish can be all of the same type, or mixtures of different types. The latter is the more usual as providing greater variety and interest, unless the pool owner wants to concentrate on breeding and raising a particular species.

Details of suitable fish types are given in Chapter 8. Once again specialist suppliers can provide balanced collections of fancy fish, selected to match specific pool sizes. This is probably the simplest and most effective, way of stocking a pool initially, especially for a beginner. Table XIII can also be used as a general guide.

For transport purposes, fish can be 'packaged' in plastic bags which are then inflated with oxygen. They can readily survive under such conditions for days or up to a week or more, even if delivered by rail or road services, when the plastic bag would be packed in an outer container. Losses in transport are usually so small as to be negligible, for fish ordered in this way.

Upon arrival—however the fish are transported from the supplier—it is essential that the water temperature in the container be equalised with that of the pool, before the fish are let free in the pool. The quickest and most effective way of doing this is usually to float the plastic bag or container, still unopened, in the pool and leave for about an hour. This will ensure that the container water temperature gradually assumes the same temperature as that of the water in the pool, when the container can be opened and the fish gently tipped out.

The shock of transferring fish from water at one temperature to water at a higher or lower temperature can cause them severe distress, or kill them, even if the temperature difference is only a matter of 5 degrees or so.

Initial Feeding

A newly stocked pool will not contain enough natural food for fish to survive. They should therefore be fed regularly with special pond fish food, and this practice should be continued throughout the first season. The golden rule in feeding is never to overfeed, as this will only make the water foul from rotting food which is left and falls to the bottom. Some fish, too, are greedy and can overeat if offered too much food. This can lead to digestive troubles developing, or even disease. It is necessary to try to find out the exact appetite of the fish, and if possible establish a regular pattern of feeding so that the fish know where and when to expect food. This is also a method of taming fish to come for food.

A fish's appetite for food should be greatest in late spring and early summer, when the pool water is warming up. It will fall off in hotter weather, and again in colder weather. During the winter months fish will probably take little food at all.

Freshly introduced fish may show a reluctance to take food sprinkled on the surface at first, in which case they should only be fed with minimum amounts, and watched to see if they are eventually attracted. Once used to the pattern of feeding, fish come readily to the feeding spot and clear food sprinkled on the surface in a matter of about five minutes. Adjust the amount dispensed to that which is all eaten up at any one time.

Suitable foods include proprietary fish foods specially prepared for pond fish, shredded shrimp and dried daphnia. High protein foods are also available which can be used as tonic foods in the spring months.

The latest development in this respect is a floating pellet fish food with high protein content which is expected to make the traditional foods like shredded shrimp and dried daphnia obsolete. One great advantage with this pelleted food is that it does not sink, however long left in the pond, so surplus can easily be removed at any time.

TABLE IX PLANTING SEASONS*

Month	Plant(s)	Remarks
January	Rock plants and dwarf shrubs	for pool surrounds only
February	Rock plants and dwarf shrubs	for pool surrounds only
March	Waterside and bog plants	for pool surrounds or in a bog pool
	Some hardy oxygenators (e.g. Hottonia)	for the pool
April	Waterside and bog plants	for pool surrounds
	Most marginal plants	
	Oxygenating plants	
May	Marginal plants	
	Oxygenating plants	
	Some water lilies*	
June	Marginal plants	
	Oxygenating plants	planted in the pool
	Water lilies	
	Miniature water lilies	
	Floating plants	
	Surface flowering plants	
July	as for June	
August	as for June except oxygenating plants	
September	Some oxygenators only (e.g. Hottonia)	
October	Dwarf conifers and rock plants	for pool surrounds
	Ferns and waterside plants	
November	as for October	for pool surrounds
December	as for October	for pool surrounds

* Plants ordered early in the season will not normally be despatched until ready for planting.

TABLE X PLANNING THE PLANT POPULATION

| Surface area of pool sq. ft. | Oxygenating* | Plant types | | Floating | Water lilies |
		Marginal	Deep marginal		
25	12	6	1 or 2	2 or 3	1
35	18	6	2	3 or 4	1 or 2
45	24	6	2 to 4	4	2
60	30	6 or 8	4 to 6	4 to 6	2 or 3
80	36	10	4 to 6	4 to 6	3
100	48	12	6 to 8	up to 10	3 or 4
120	60	12 to 16	8 to 10	up to 12	4 or 5
General rule per 10 sq. ft. surface area	5 or 6	2 (but reduce in larger pools	1 or 2	1	†

* A vigorous variety such as Crowfoot or Water Thyme, together with Startwort for its winter activity, is particularly recommended for basic stock plants.

† In the case of water lilies, work on the basis that each lily needs about 25 sq. ft. of surface area to develop properly. Suitable varieties must be chosen for the planting depth available.

TABLE XI RECOMMENDED PLANT CONTAINER
SIZES (usually made in polythene)

8″×8″×4″ deep for	10″×10″×6″ deep for	12″×12″×8″ deep for
Marginals	Deep Marginals	Deep marginals
Oxygenating plants	Oxygenating plants	Water lilies
Miniature lilies	Water lilies	

TABLE XII ALTERNATIVE CONTENTS FOR
PLANT CONTAINERS

8″×8″×4″ (or near size)	10″×10″×6″ (or near size)	12″×12″×8″ (or near size)
4–6 oxygenating plants or 1 marginal or 1 miniature lily	12–16 oxygenating plants or 2–3 marginals or 2 deep marginals or 1 water lily	3 marginals or 3 deep marginals or 1 water lily

TABLE XIII FISH POPULATION GUIDE

Pool surface area (sq. ft.)	2–3" fish	3–4" fish	Collection of 5–6" fish	Scavengers*
15	10	—	—	—
25	10	6 to 8	—	1
35	12	8	2	1 or 2
45	12	8 to 10	2 to 4	2
60	up to 20	10 to 15	4 to 6	2
80	up to 25	15 to 20	6 to 8	2 or 3
100	up to 30	up to 20	8 or 10	3

* Not essential

7

Plants for the Garden Pool

Species of plants suitable for the garden pool are so numerous that they could well form the subject of a separate book. Basic types, characteristics and planting seasons have already been described in Chapter 6. This chapter is intended mainly as a reference for plant names, arranged under types. In each group listing is in alphabetical order of botanical names, this normally being adopted by the specialist suppliers. Common names are given in brackets following, where applicable. It should also be noted that as far as general requirements are concerned, plants may also be ordered and supplied by *type* name. For example, ordering a certain number of *oxygenating plants,* any one of a dozen species might well be supplied, or a mixture of these. The usefulness of this chapter is that it enables the individual pond owner to be more selective; but similar listings will also be found in suppliers' catalogues.

OXYGENATING PLANTS

Oxygenating plants are normally available from March to August, this depending to some extent on species. They are generally unsuitable for planting after mid-August, in any case. Besides providing oxygen, they help to keep algae growth in check, as well as providing food for the fish. Clusters of oxygenating plants are also good spawning ground for fish.

The general recommendation is one oxygenating plant for every 2 square feet of pond surface area. However, in a new pool this density could be doubled,

thinning out at the end of the first season. One important point often overlooked is that to behave as active
oxygenators these submerged plants need light. They
should therefore not be planted in parts of the pool
where they can become fully shaded by larger plants
with floating leaves.

Anachris—see *Elodea*

Callitriche
There are two main sub-species—*verna* (Starwort)
and *autumnalis* (Water Starwort). The latter is one
of the few oxygenators which remains active during
the winter months but is not particularly effective.
Threadlike stems with neat green foliage.

Ceratophyllum demersum (Hornwort)
Branching stems with dark green narrow leaves in the
shape of whorls. Will grow without being planted,
only in this case it is recommended that the bottom
of the stem be weighted.

Eleocharis acicularis (Hair Grass)
Thin threadlike leaves of pale to mid green.

Elodea canadensis (Water Thyme)
Strong vigorous growth and a very active oxygenator.

Elodea crispa
Also known as Water Thyme or Curled Thyme, or
Curled Anachris, because of its reflex leaf shape. Other-
wise as for *canadensis*.

Fontanalis antipyretica (Willow Moss)
Abundant, soft dark green foliage. May need weighting
down to keep on the bottom. This plant prefers a
shady location in the pool.

Myriophyllum spicatum (Water Milfoil)
Long stems with fine green, olive green, or sometimes
bronze foliage. A less active oxygenator.

Potamogeton crispus (Pondweed)
Rather like curly edged seaweed in appearance, with leaves varying in colour from green to bronze. A very active oxygenator.

Ranunculus aquatilis (Water Crowfoot)
An excellent oxygenator which also grows up through the surface of the water yielding waving green foliage and an abundance of white flowers in June–July (*see illustration*).

Vallisneria spiralis (Eel Grass or Tape Grass)
Light green, twisted ribbon-like leaves growing from a central crown. This is one of the few oxygenating plants which develops a proper root system, but is not entirely hardy.

FLOATING PLANTS

These plants merely float on the surface of the water and are useful for providing shade, and decoration, provided they are not allowed to propagate too extensively. If used in a pool which has a fountain or waterfall they will naturally be swept to the more static regions of the pool surface, where they will bunch up.

Azolla caroliniana (Fairy Moss or Floating Moss)
Really a miniature floating fern. Colours range from light green, changing to pink, bronze or red during the autumn. Propagates readily and may need to be kept under control by thinning out.

Eichhornia crassipes (Floating Water Hyacinth)
Develops a bulbous base with hanging roots and throws up delicate pale violet flowers on spikes. Rather sensitive to conditions and cannot survive frost, so must be wintered in an indoor pool.

Hydrocharis morsus-ranae (Frogbit)
Dark green leaves with hanging stems, rather like those of a miniature water lily. Bears a profusion of small white flowers in July and August (*see illustration*).

Lemna minor (Duckweed)
Small bright green leaves which rapidly develop a carpet covering over the surface. Useful as a fish food, but needs thinning out regularly because of its rapid propagation during the summer months.

Lemna trisulca (Ivy-leaved Duckweed)
Attractive translucent pale green leaves which normally remain submerged, except for limited periods during the summer when they rise and float on the surface.

Stratiotes aloides (Water Soldier).
Swordlike dark green leaves radiating from a crown with hanging roots. This plant normally winters on the bottom but rises to the surface in summer, when it develops white flowers carried on short stalks (*see illustration*).

Utricularia vulgaris (Bladderwort)
A small plant developing long wiry underwater stems. Winters submerged but rises to the surface in summer and throws up small bright yellow flowers. Submerges again in August. Requires acid waters to survive.

DEEP MARGINALS

These are plants suitable for growing in deeper water, usually up to 12 inches, and throwing up foliage and flowers above the surface. They are chosen mainly for decoration.

Alisma natans (Water Plantain)
A small plant with dainty leaves, developing small white flowers in the summer. Mainly suitable for small pools.

Aponogeton distachyum (Water Hawthorn)
Develops oval-shaped floating green leaves and flowers freely from April onwards. The flowers are white with black anthers, and scented. Thrives in most pools and prefers deeper water (up to 20 inches).

63

Hottonia palustris (Water Violet)
Fernlike foliage which remains below the water surface,
throwing up long stems carrying white or pale violet
flowers 6 to 12 inches above the surface. Rather a
tricky plant to grow, but also recommended as an
oxygenator (*see illustration*).

Orontium aquaticum (Golden Club)
Needs planting in deep soil (10–12 inches should be
regarded as a minimum), with 4 to 10 inches of water
above the soil. Attractive foliage throwing up slender
yellow flowers (*see illustration*).

Villarsia bennetti
Like a minature water lily, developing attractive
yellow flowers and a multiplicity of floating leaves
(*see illustration*).

Villarsia nymphaliodes (Floating Heart or Bean Lily)
Similar species with dark green leaves lightly mottled
with red or brown. Bright yellow flowers.

WATER LILIES

Water lilies are the aristocrats of aquatic plants, and
also the most expensive. Individual plants may cost from
about 12s. (60p) up to several pounds each. Once established a water lily should flower continuously throughout the summer, the petals of each flower closing at
night. The planting season usually starts in mid or
late April and can continue through until September.
    There are various ways of classifying water lilies,
but the most significant is the vigour of their growth
since this largely determines the depth of water in
which they should be planted. Most varieties culti-
vated for pools are of moderate to medium vigour,
suitable for water depths of 12 to 24 inches. Miniature

water lilies may be happy in as little as 3 inches of water.

The number of varieties in cultivation is high, emphasis also being placed on hardiness as well as controlled vigour. The specialist suppliers invariably give depth of water required, but this can still vary somewhat for the same name lily between different suppliers, largely because of differences in cultivation. It is thus impossible to give any complete overall guide.

The following is a typical listing from one supplier (Highlands Water Gardens), together with recommendations for planting depth. This figure refers to the depth of water above the soil in which the lily is planted, with the crown just above the soil.

Key: *a* for water 15 to 36 inches deep
b for water 10 to 24 inches deep
c for water 7 to 15 inches deep
d for water 3 to 10 inches deep

Red, carmine and crimson shades

ab Attraction
Flowers carmine, maturing to glowing garnet-red, with white sepals; robust and prolific.

a Charles de Meurville
Large blooms open pink and mature to deep wine-red; very vigorous.

bc Conqueror
A prolific and attractive lily with large cup-shaped flowers of glowing rose-crimson.

b Escarboucle
The best of the reds, and regarded by many as the most desirable of all water lilies. Large, crimson flowers of perfect shape, very freely produced. Unequalled for richness of colour.

cd Froebeli
A small lily that produces bright red flowers in lavish profusion; perfect for small pools.

bc **Gloriosa**
This scarce beauty originated in America, where it
is the favourite red lily. The wide-opening flowers
are rich red and delightfully scented.

bc **James Brydon**
Splendid cup-shaped flowers of carmine-red;
leaves purple, maturing to green; prolific.

cd **Laydekeri purpurata**
A first-class lily for shallow pools; flowers crimson,
maturing to dark red.

b **Newton**
Large star-shaped blooms, often lifted above the
water; the bright cherry-red petals contrast vividly
with unusually long bright golden stamens.

b **Rembrandt**
A vigorous lily with handsome blooms, wine-pink,
maturing to currant-red.

bc **Rene Gerard**
Shapely flowers, freely produced, rose-red deepening to wine-splashed crimson.

Pink and rose shades

bc **Firecrest**
A lovely flower with deep clear pink petals and
striking orange-tipped stamens.

bc **Irene**
A beautiful new variety with starry flowers of clear
rich rose-pink; a valuable acquisition.

cd **Laydekeri lilacea**
A pleasing pink for small pools; blooms mature
from lilac to carmine.

cd **Laydekeri rosea**
The rarest and loveliest of the small lilies; the
perfectly shaped deep rose-pink blooms are
fragrant, and abundantly produced.

bc *Lustrous*
A free-flowering American favourite of unique colour—rose-pink with a lovely silvery sheen.

bc *Mme. Wilfron Gonnere*
Beautiful flowers of rich pink; the shape and arrangement of the petals recalls the beauty of the finest double camellias.

bc *Marliacea rosea*
Robust and prolific, the flowers (often white at first) are suffused with light rose.

ab *Masaniello*
Large paeony-shaped blooms, rose-pink, with the centre deepening to rich carmine.

b *Mrs. Richmond*
Very large flowers, plentifully produced, deep pink and maturing to an even richer shade in the centre; green foliage. Deservedly popular.

bc *Odorata rosea*
Beautiful rose-pink blooms with a delicate fragrance; robust and prolific.

c *Odorata turicensis*
A charming medium-sized lily with abundant starry soft pink scented blooms.

bc *Odorata W. B. Shaw*
Delightful shell-pink blooms lifted above the surface; deliciously perfumed.

bc *Rose Arey*
Cerise-pink petals, pointed and incurved; has more scent than any other variety, and a strong claim to being the finest of the pink varieties.

White Lilies

bc *Albatross*
Snow-white blooms with golden stamens, set off by apple-green leaves; very pleasing.

67

cd *Candida*
Charming small flowers with yellow centres; a very satisfactory lily for small pools.

ab *Gladstoniana*
Immense cup-shaped flowers of purest white, with gleaming gold stamens; superb.

bc *Gonnere* (Crystal White)
Large very double flowers of outstanding beauty; the globular blooms, crowded with curving petals, make this a uniquely charming and attractive variety.

bc *Marliacea albida*
Sparkling white blooms with yellow stamens; sepals tinted pink; prolific.

bc *Odorata alba*
Delightfully scented white flowers and attractive light green foliage.

cd *Odorata minor*
A perfect choice for small pools and shallow water, with scented star-shaped flowers.

d *Pygmaea alba*
A dainty and prolific miniature lily with small snow-white flowers and green leaves; ideal for the smallest pools and very shallow water.

ab *Tuberosa Richardsoni*
Vigorous grower with splendid white blooms and pea-green sepals.

Yellow, orange and coppery shades

cd *Aurora*
Soft buff-yellow flowers, maturing to deep apricot; prettily mottled foliage; unusual.

ab *Colonel Welch*
A vigorous grower, with canary-yellow flowers, standing well out of the water.

cd Graziella
Yellow flowers suffused reddish copper, and becoming lighter with age; leaves marked purple.

bc Indiana
Very changeable flowers, deepening from pale reddish orange to rich copper-red; mottled foliage.

bc Marliacea chromatella (Golden Cup)
Large yellow blooms and attractively mottled foliage.

bc Odorata sulphurea grandiflora
Elegant star-shaped flowers, a richer colour than most yellows, held above the water; one of the most pleasing lilies.

d Pygmaea helvola
A delightful and very prolific dwarf lily with yellow flowers and small mottled leaves. The best of the miniatures.

bc Sunrise
This glorious American variety is supreme among the yellow lilies for colour and size of blooms, with the added virtue of delicious fragrance.

MARGINAL PLANTS

These are so numerous that any complete listing is impossible. The following are types likely to be available from most specialist suppliers and are taken from a listing by Bennett's Water Lily and Fish Farm.

Acorus calamus (Sweet-scented Rush)
Erect sword-like green foliage. Height 2 feet. Depth 3 inches to 5 inches.

Acorus calamus variegatus
A very striking plant. Green and yellow foliage. Height 2 feet. Depth 3 inches to 5 inches.

Acorus gramineus variegatus
Variegated form of dwarf Japanese rush. Height 9 inches. Depth of water 1 inch to 2 inches.

Alisma plantago (Water Plantain)
Small pink and white flowers. Height 2 feet. Damp soil to 6 inches deep (*see illustration*).

Butomus umbellatus (Flowering Rush)
Rose-pink flowers, 3 inches to 5 inches deep. Height 2½ feet (*see illustration*).

Calla palustris (Bog Arum)
White flowers, 2 inches to 4 inches deep water. Height 6 inches.

Caltha palustris (Marsh Marigold or Kingcup)
Bright golden yellow, flowers in early spring. Height 1 foot. Best in wet soil or in water up to 3 inches (*see illustration*).

Caltha palustris alba
A white variety from the Himalayas.

Caltha palustris plena (Double Marsh Marigold)
Very double variety of the yellow variety above.

Cotula coronopifolia (Golden Buttons)
Excellent for small or large ponds. Covered the whole summer and even into early winter with small yellow, button-like flowers. Height 9 inches. Damp soil to 5 inches deep water.

Cyperus longus (Sweet Galingale)
Ornamental rush. Height 2 feet 3 inches to 5 inches of water. Sought after by members of floral decoration societies.

Eriophorum angustifolium (Cotton Grass)
Terminates in conspicuous white silky tufts. Height 12 to 14 inches. Plant in deep water.

Glyceria spectabilis variegata
Prettily striped grass. Plant 2 inches to 5 inches deep.
Grows 2 feet tall.

Iris kaempferi. Large-flowered, moisture-loving irises,
equally at home on the edge of a pool, just in water, or
in a moist position outside the pool; 1½ feet. The
beautiful clematis-flowered iris of Japan.

Iris kaempferi higo strain
Recently imported from Japan. In mixed colours
only. Creates a real show of colour with double flowers
up to 10 inches in diameter.

Iris kaempferi variegata
Rich purple flowers which contrast pleasingly with
green and cream striped foliage. Height 2 feet.

Iris laevigata. This family of Japanese water iris is
completely trouble-free and grows in wet soil or a
few inches of water. They flower in June and usually
again in late September.

Iris laevigata
The original variety, is considered by many authorities
to be the finest type of iris in cultivation. Height 1½
feet, water 2 inches to 4 inches deep.

Iris laevigata atropurpurea
Vivid blue form of laevigata. Height 1½ feet. Depth
2 inches to 4 inches.

Iris laevigata monsrosa
Flowers strikingly marked in blue and white.

Iris laevigata, Rose Queen
A cross between iris laevigata and iris kaempferi.
Thrives better in moist soil than in a few inches of
water. Flowers a pleasing pink.

Iris laevigata variegata
Pleasing variegated foliage, flowers blue.

Iris pseudacorus (Yellow Water Iris)
Best in damp soil or up to 6 inches deep.

Iris pseudacorus bastardi
Rare lemon yellow form of above.

Iris pseudacorus variegata
Variegated form of yellow iris above.

Iris sibirica, Emperor
Dark blue with yellow centre. Height 2 feet, damp soil only (*see illustration*).

Iris sibirica, Heavenly Blue
Damp soil only. Height 2 feet.

Iris sibirica, Snow Queen
White flower with yellow centre. Height 2 feet.

Iris versicolor
Distinctive, variegated blooms of rich claret, blue and yellow. Height 18 inches. Depth 2 inches to 4 inches.

Lysichitum americanum
Large leaves, yellow flowers. Wet soil only. Height 2 feet.

Lysichitum camschatense
White Japanese variety.

Mentha aquatica (Water Mint)
Sweetly smelling foliage and deep lilac-coloured flowers. Damp soil to 3 inches deep. Height 9 inches (*see illustration*).

Menyanthes trifoliata (Bog Bean)
Bean-like leaves, pinkish flowers, 2 inches to 4 inches deep. Height 9 inches.

Mimulus luteus (Yellow Monkey Musk)
Small yellow flowers, spotted red. Wet soil to 3 inches deep water. Height 1 foot.

Minulus luteus
Hose in hose. One bloom forms within another in a most fascinating manner, growth and details as above.

Mimulus ringens (Lavender Musk)
3 inches to 5 inches deep water. Height 18 inches.

Mimulus, Whitecroft Scarlet
Damp soil only. Bright scarlet. Height 4 inches.
Does not grow in water.

Myosotis palustris (Water Forget-me-Not)
A deeper blue and longer lasting than the dry soil
variety. Height 6 inches. Damp soil or up to 3 inches
deep.

Myriophyllum proserpinacoides (Parrot's Feather)
A submerged aquatic plant which pokes its graceful
head 6 inches above the surface of the water. Plant in
3 inches to 6 inches of water.

Pontederia cordata (Pickerel)
Flowers like a small blue delphinium, handsome
foliage. 3 inches to 5 inches of water. Height 1½ feet
(*see illustration*).

Ranunculus lingua grandiflora (Great Spearwort)
Yellow flowers. Height 2 feet. Plant 3 inches to 6 inches
deep.

Sagittaria japonica (Arrowhead, Japanese variety)
Foliage extremely arrow-shaped. Pleasing white flowers
with yellow centres.

Sagittaria japonica plena (Arrowhead, Double Japanese
variety)
White flowers resembling a gigantic double stock with
arrow-shaped leaves which give the plant its name.
3 inches to 5 inches deep. Height 1 foot (*see illustration*).

Sagittaria sagittifolia (Arrowhead, Common variety)
Interesting arrowhead-haped leaves, white flowers with
black centres. 3 inches to 5 inches deep. Height 1 foot
(*see illustration*).

Scirpus albescens
Green and white vertical variegated foliage. Height
3 feet. Water 2 inches to 4 inches deep.

Scirpus holoschoenus
A true bulrush. N.B. Typha below. Height 1 foot to 2 feet. Best in damp soil or up to 6 inches deep.

Scirpus zebrinus (Zebra Rush)
A very striking, attractive and desirable rush. Height 2½ feet. 3 inches to 5 inches deep (*see illustration*).

Sparganium ramosum (Bur-reed)
A green rush with prickly flowers. Height 2 feet. Water 3 inches to 5 inches deep.

Typha angustifolia
(All 'typhas' have brown, poker-like heads and are usually, but erroneously, known as bulrush.) Slender graceful leaves, dark brown, slender poker heads. Height 3 feet. Damp soil to 6 inches deep water (*see illustration*).

Typha latifolia (Great Reed-Mace)
Large brown cat's-tail spikes. Height 4 feet.

Typha minima
A dwarf Japanese variety of the above. Height only 1½ feet. Damp soil or up to 4 inches deep.

Typha stenophylla (Small Reed-Mace)
Brown cat's-tail spikes. Height 3 feet. Best in damp soil or up to 6 inches deep.

Veronica beccabunga (Brooklime)
Blue flowers. Height 6 inches. Water 0 inches to 4 inches deep.

BOG PLANTS

Most of the marginal plants will thrive equally well in permanently damp soil, as well as submerged soil, and so can be used for planting in a bog garden.

Certain plants, however, will not grow in water, but only in saturated soil. These are the true bog plants, which include bog primulas and other types.

Asthore hybrids (Bog Primula)
Usually orange, but may also be pink or mauve.

74

Aurantiaca (Bog Primula)
Growing to a height of 9 inches, with orange red flower.

Bulleyna (Bog Primula)
Larger plants growing to a height of 18 inches. Dull orange flowers in May and June. There are also several hybrids of this species with pink or red flowers.

Burmanica (Bog Primula)
Dark red flowers tinged with yellow-gold in June.

Calthas (Marsh Marigold)
Height up to 6 inches. Marigold yellow flowers. May to June.

Denticulata (Bog Primula)
Height 12 inches. Large white or lilac flowers in March and April.

Florindae (Bog Primula)
Height up to 24 inches. Yellow flowers June and August.

Iris kaempferi (Iris)
All varieties and colours. Heights from 24 to 36 inches. Flowering May to July, according to variety (*see illustration*).

Japonica (Bog Primula)
Height 18 inches. White, pink or red flowers in May and June.

Lysimachia nummularia (Creeping Jenny)
Spreading growth, ideal for pool edges. Height about 2 inches. Develops yellow flowers and prefers shade.

Mentha aquatica (Water Mint)
Grows to a height of 9 inches with clusters of lilac flowers in summer. Leaves if pinched have a smell of mint.

Menyanthes trifoliata (Bog Bean)
Another edging plant with creeping growth. Height 9 inches. Smooth olive green leaves. White flowers tinged with pink in May to June.

Mimulus luteus
Height 12 inches, developing yellow flowers in the summer.

Mysotis palustris (Water Forget-Me-Not)
Height 6 inches. Small blue flowers in summer.

Molinia caerulea variegata
Dwarf ornamental grass with white striped green leaves growing to a height of 12 inches.

Peltiphyllum peltatum (Umbrella Plant)
Grows to a height of 18 inches with large, wide shiny dark green leaves. Pink flowers in April.

Phalaris arundinacea (Gardener's Garters)
Striped grassy foliage growing to a height of 18 inches.

Pulverulenta (Bog Primula)
Height 24 inches. Pink flowers in June and July.

Rosea grandiflora (Bog Primula)
Height 6 inches. Pink flowers in April.

Veronica beccabunga (Creeping Brooklime).
Height 6 inches. Shiny dark green foliage with small blue flowers.

WATERSIDE PLANTS

These differ from bog plants in that they will not grow in waterlogged soil but can be used to form attractive borders around the edge of a pool. The following is a partial list from Garden Pools Ltd.

Key: *a*—suitable for normal garden soil with average moisture content (watering needed in dry weather).

m—suitable for soil which receives ample moisture in summer (e.g. frequent waterings), but is not waterlogged. Ideal for the banks of natural pools and streams.

am *Anchusa caespitosa*
Intense gentian-blue flowers; a striking plant;
May–September; 1½ feet.

m *Aruncus (Spiraea) sylvester kneiffi* (Goat's Beard)
Plumes of creamy white; June–July; 3 feet.

m *Astilbe chinensis minima*
Dwarf; rose-pink; 9 inches (*see illustration*).

m *Astilbe europa*
Spikes of flesh-pink; 3 feet.

m *Astilbe Gertrude Brix*
Deep red; June–July; 2½ feet.

m *Astilbe Fanal*
Brilliant red; 2 feet.

m *Astilbe W. E. Gladstone*
Perfect white; 2½ feet.

am *Bergenia delavayi* (Elephant's Ears)
Colourful evergreen leaves; pink flowers; April–
May; 1½ feet.

am *Bergenia Dayblush*
Bright pink flowers produced freely; spring *and*
autumn; 10 inches.

am *Bergenia Evening Glow*
Compact growth; bronzy autumn colour; purple-
red flowers; 12 inches.

am *Bergenia Silverlight*
Flowers white with a pearly pink glow; excellent
foliage; 1½ feet.

am *Coreopsis Rubythroat*
Useful dwarf plant for waterside or rockery;
brown-centred, yellow flowers; 9 inches.

am *Coreopsis Sunchild*
Bright yellow flowers; cheerful colour over long
season; 14 inches.

77

am Dicentra Adrian Bloom
Crimson flowers April–May; pretty foliage; out standing; 12 inches.

am Dicentra spectabilis (Bleeding Heart)
Very popular; rosy crimson flowers; May–July; 2 feet.

am Festuca glauca
Silvery blue foliage; 6 inches.

am Geum borisi
Dark evergreen leaves; bright orange-yellow flowers. May–July; 9 inches.

am Hemerocallis Dark Flame (Day Lily)
New variety; mahogany-red blooms; July–August; 1½ feet (*see illustration*).

am Hemerocallis George Yeld
Large pure yellow blooms; 2 feet.

am Hemerocallis tejas
Copper-red with yellow centre.

am Hemerocallis kwanso plena variegata
Double orange-red flowers; boldly variegated; leaves 3 feet.

am Hosta (Funkia)
Group of plants with handsome foliage, striking in colour, form, and texture. Invaluable for waterside planting; much in demand by flower arrangers (*see illustration*).

am Hosta fortunei
Large glaucous leaves; lilac flowers; 2 feet.

am Hosta albo-picta
Large leaves boldly marked with yellow; 2 feet.

am Hosta lancifolia albo-marginata
Bold green leaves edged with white; mauve flowers; 1½ feet.

Stepping stones are always an attraction where the pool is large enough to accommodate them.

Large pools like this are perfectly within the scope of do-it-yourself construction, using flexible pool liner material.

Two examples of round shaped pools, both planned to give an attractive overall effect. The steps down to the smaller pool are particularly effective. The larger pool blends into a planted area of the garden.

Two examples of pools designed as part of a walled feature. The half-round pool is built up above ground level with stones. The larger circular pool with stepping stones across adds to the attraction of the moongate.

Well-planned formal pool with four fountain sprays and central figure ornament.

This photograph shows how perfectly natural a plastic-lined pool can be made to look.

(Photo courtesy of Bennetts' Water Lily and Fish Farm.)

am *Hosta sieboldiana*
Large glaucous foliage, deeply veined; pale lilac flowers; 2 feet.

am *Hosta undulata variegata*
Particularly attractive leaves, dark green splashed with paler green and cream; 1½ feet.

am *Ligularia (senecio) clivorum*
Orange-yellow flowers; handsome leaves; July–September; 3 feet.

m *Lobelia vedariense*
Unusual violet-blue variety; 2 feet.

m *Mimulus A. T. Johnson*
Bright yellow, marked reddish brown; prolific; June–September; 1 foot.

m *Mimulus bartonianus*
Rose-pink; 2 feet.

m *Mimulus burnetti*
Vivid bronze-orange; 9 inches.

m *Mimulus cardinalis*
Showy crimson flowers; 1½ feet.

m *Mimulus langsdorfii alpinus*
Brightest yellow; 9 inches.

m *Mimulus Red Emperor*
Richest red variety; 6 inches.

m *Mimulus Scarlet Bee*
Intense scarlet; 6 inches.

m *Miscanthus sinensis*
Bamboo-like perennial for bold groups or screening; feathery flower panicles; 5 feet.

am *Monarda Pillar Box*
Bright red flower spikes; 3 feet.

am *Potentilla Gibson's Scarlet*
Vivid red flowers, free and continuous; June–Aug.

am *Pulmonaria officinalis*
Silver spotted foliage, pink and blue flowers.
March–April. 9 inches.

am *Pulmonaria saccharata azurea*
The best blue. 9 inches.

m *Ranunculus acontifolius plenus* (Fair Maids of
France)
Double white blooms. May–June. Height 1 foot.

am *Rheum Palmatum Tanguticum*
Rhubarb-like leaves, deeply lobed; imposing
crimson flower panicle. 3 feet.

am *Rodgersia aesculifolia*
Fine foliage plant; branched panicles of white
blossom. 2 feet.

am *Rodgersia tabularis*
Large, almost round leaves; creamy white flower
plumes. 3 feet.

a *Salvia East Friesland*
15 inch spikes of lovely violet-blue flowers through
summer.

m *Saxifraga fortunei Wada's Form*
Splendid plant for moist spot; white flowers. The
main and season-long attraction is lush, rich
purple foliage.

am *Sidalcea Brilliant*
Splendid pink flower spikes. 2½ feet.

Tradescantial. Fine group of moisture-loving,
shade-tolerant plants. Flowers non-stop June–
September. 15 inches.

am *Tradescantia Leonora*
Large clear blue flowers.

am *Tradescantia Osprey*
White flowers, fluffy light blue centres.

am *Tradescantia rubra*
Deep reddish purple flowers.

m   *Trollius First Lancers*
    Deep orange flowers. $2\frac{1}{2}$ feet.

m   *Trollius Golden Queen*
    One of the finest Globe Flowers; rich golden
    blooms. May–June. 2 feet.

m   *Trollius Orange Princess*
    Brilliant orange. 2 feet.

Although not listed, *ferns* can also be considered as
suitable waterside plants for decoration. These are best
located in shady, moist positions, but where the soil
has ample drainage. Certain species will only grow in a
wet position. Dwarf conifers are another good choice
for pool surrounds.

*Plant illustrations in this chapter by courtesy of Stewarts (Ferndown)
Nurseries Ltd.*

8

Fish for Garden Pools

Pond fish need to be hardy for they have to withstand quite severe changes in water temperature—from freezing point in winter (32 degrees F.), up to a range of 50 to 70 degrees F. in the summer months. Also both the acidity and hardness of the water may undergo changes. As a consequence freshwater fish which naturally live in running streams, or large lakes, seldom thrive in an artificial pool. The choice therefore becomes more or less limited to the fish bred specially for smaller pools. The emphasis here is also on colour and attractive appearance, as well as suitability, which is why such types are often called 'fancy fish' or, ornamental fish. These will be described under separate headings.

Goldfish
These are the best known of all ornamental fish, and also the hardiest. The goldfish has also been bred and interbred to such an extent that there are now a considerable number of varieties other than the familiar 'gold' fish with its streamlined body and compact fins and tail. What is also little known is that under ideal conditions a goldfish may live for twenty years or more and attain a length, perhaps, of 18 inches. However, ideal conditions in this case means lots of space as well as a properly balanced pond. Whilst goldfish may be long-lived in the typical garden pool, they would not normally be expected to grow to more than 8 to 12 inches long, and many will not even achieve 6 inches.

The name *goldfish* is generally applied to fish having a gold or red-coloured body, regardless of whether this is marked with black or not. An overall gold (no black markings) would properly be described as pure gold—but in the case of a breeding pair may still produce offspring with black markings. Variations on the gold colour, such as silver, yellow, pearl-white, and so on—again with or without additional markings—are generally referred to as *fancy colours*.

Goldfish are the 'basic' stock of any garden pool, and also the least expensive. They can be bought in sizes from 2 inches body length upwards. Anything smaller is too young to be introduced into totally new surroundings without risking a high mortality rate. This basic recommendation, in fact, applies to practically all ornamental fish.

Shubunkins

These are close relatives of the goldfish, with non-shiny translucent scales. Their colours are more varied than goldfish and include yellows, reds, blues, browns and various mottled varieties. So great is the colouring variety that the appearance of a shubunkin can range from very attractive to dull and lifeless-looking. The most satisfactory specimens are usually those picked out to personal choice. The more attractive varieties, however, are likely to be more highly priced.

Shubunkins are equally as hardy as true goldfish and are even more readily tamed. That is, they can be trained to come to a certain part of the pool for food and can eventually be made to take food from the fingers or hand.

Nymphs

This is another variety of goldfish with a deep, rounded body and with long fins and tail. Colour is usually a rich deep golden red.

Comets

This is the general description given to ornamental fish with long, flowing tails. The chief varieties are Comet Longtail Goldfish, and Comet Longtail Shubunkins, with all the colour variations of the basic species. They are generally about twice as expensive as the short-tailed varieties, size for size, and can be regarded as just as hardy.

Calicos

This description is given to fish with fan-shaped tails, often with large, graceful fin shapes to match. Here the varieties available are more limited, the most usual being Calico Shubunkin Fantails. In some cases the name 'fantail' is used, particularly when referring to a specific body colour—e.g. Red Fantail.

Both Comets and Fantails (Calicos) are best suited for small- and medium sized pools, but are rather susceptible to disease such as Tail Rot.

Carp

The carp is a well-known freshwater fish of somewhat aggressive nature. Carp are really only suited to large pools, since they can grow to considerable size. The two varieties regarded as ornamental fish are the *mirror carp* and the *higoi golden carp*. The mirror carp is yellowish grey in colour with a deep, arched body and large head. The higoi golden carp is overall gold in colour and more attractive in appearance.

Neither type should be introduced into a small- or medium-sized pool.

Golden Orfe

This is an attractive fish, similar in size and shape to a goldfish, but with a less deep gold colour running into silver. Fins may sometimes be flecked with red, and black markings may also be found on some varieties. Orfe without any gold colouring are called *silver orfe*.

Orfe are very active fish, darting vigorously about the pool. They are basically top swimmers, that is, they like to live mainly near the surface, and will also take small insects and flies from the water surface. Because they use up a lot of energy they need plenty of oxygen. When orfe are obviously off colour and sluggish, it may well be an indication that the water is getting foul and starved of oxygen. Otherwise they are extremely hardy fish and will take almost any food. They are happiest in medium- or larger-sized pools which are not overcrowded so that they have plenty of freedom of movement.

Golden Rudd

Similar to the orfe, but rather deeper in body and far less active. When happily settled in they spend most of their time cruising up and down the pond in middle waters, although they do visit the surface. Colouring is bronze-gold on top, thinning out to a more silvery or even greenish underbody. Fin extremities may be marked in red. Colour toning is much more attractive in some specimens than others.

Green Tench

This fish is a scavenger, living at the bottom of the pool and seldom, if ever, even venturing up as far as middle waters. It is a useful addition to any pond, but once introduced will probably not be seen again.

Other varieties

The above covers all the main varieties of ornamental fish usually considered suitable for garden pools. Mixed collections are capable of living together in harmony (with the possible exception of the carp once it attains a reasonable size); and so there is no problem with regard to which fish goes with which in selecting a collection.

Specialist suppliers may offer additional species to those named, and in such cases can give advice on their suitability. The main thing to avoid is introducing *coldwater aquarium fish* into an outdoor pool, as they are hardly likely to survive, with the possible exception of the Black Moor.

Coarse fish

Coarse fish—or natural fresh water river fish—are, in general, regarded as unsuitable for garden pools, not only because of their lack of colour, but because of their predatory habits. Also with fish caught from rivers or streams there is always a danger of introducing infection into the pool. Nevertheless, certain species may be regarded as 'suitable', especially when obtained from specialist suppliers. The Carp, Silver Orfe, Rudd and Tench have already been mentioned. All these are strictly speaking 'coarse' fish rather than 'fancy' fish, even if bred specially for garden pools. Other species of coarse fish which may be considered include Minnows and Sticklebacks. Trout, incidentally, are quite unsuitable for garden pools.

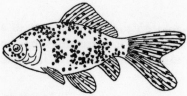

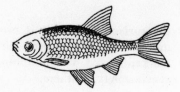

Shubunkins
Very good pond variety with non-shining scales, giving mother-of-pearl effect to the colouring.

Golden and Silver Rudd
Both have red-tinted fins. Golden variety has reddish body colour. Surface feeders, suitable for larger pools.

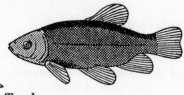

Comet Longtail
Variants of both goldfish and shubunkins with abnormally long tails and fins.

Tench
Useful scavengers of drowned worms, and food fragments.

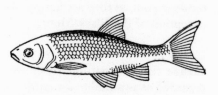

Nymphs
Lovely fish with short, rounded bodies and extremely graceful large tails.

Golden and Silver Orfe
Lively, darting, slender fish—the former salmon orange and the latter silver—of more active habit than goldfish.

Goldfish
Normally red-gold Fancy-coloured goldfish may be yellow or pearly white, or marked with combinations of black, silver, yellow, white or red.

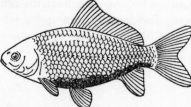

Fish illustrations by courtesy of Highlands Water Gardens Ltd.

9

Care and Breeding of Fish

Healthy fish will normally live happily for years in a properly balanced pool and so the incidence of disease should be comparatively uncommon. However, such troubles can arise—the cause normally being a pool which has been allowed to get into a very bad condition, or the introduction into the pool of a fish which is already suffering from some infectious disease. The latter emphasises the importance of buying only good 'stock', from a reputable supplier.

Disease in pond fish is usually most likely to show up in the spring or early summer months, particularly when the resources of the fish have been drained to a low level by a hard winter. Troubles should be watched for regularly, for they can start at any time, and if a fish can be identified as having contracted a disease it should be removed at once—either for treatment, or to be destroyed. This does not necessarily apply where the fish is merely sluggish or apparently out of condition. This may simply be due to a temporary unbalance of the pool conditions, or a seasonal habit. Here the cure is to treat the pool rather than the fish— see Chapter 10.

Fungus Disease
This is a disease caused by poor water conditions and contrary to popular belief is not contagious, although more than one fish in the pool may be affected. Fortunately it is comparatively rare on healthy fish and is normally likely to develop only on weak fish in a poor state of health to start with, or to fish which have been injured. Here it should be noted that even handling a fish with dry fingers can injure it.

Fungus disease is noted by a white woolly growth which first appears on the side of the fish and, if unchecked, can spread to cover the whole of its body. Provided the attack can be recognised at an early stage there is every hope of curing it. If the disease has already spread over a considerable proportion of the body, probably the best thing to do is to remove it and destroy it.

For treatment, two separate tanks are required—such as large goldfish bowls or small indoor aquariums. Failing anything else, two ordinary buckets will do. One should be filled with fresh water and the other with salt solution made up by dissolving about half a cupful of domestic salt in each gallon of water. These tanks should be stood near the pool and left until their water temperatures are the same as that of the pool. Use a thermometer to check when this is so.

The diseased fish is then removed with a net and transferred to the salt solution. It can be left in this for up to twenty minutes, or such a time that it shows obvious distress. It should then be removed from the salt solution and placed in the tank or container holding the fresh water. Aerate the water by playing a hose on the surface until the fish shows signs of recovering its normal activity. It can then be left in the separate fresh water tank, which can be placed in a suitable protected place.

This treatment should be continued daily, checking each time first that the temperatures of the salt and fresh waters are the same before transferring the fish from one to the other. After the cure has been completed the fish should still be kept in isolation, in fresh water, for a further few days before returning to the pool.

Where more than one or two fish are affected by the disease the cause may be unsuitable pond conditions lowering the state of health of the inhabitants. One possibility is that the water is too hard and alkaline. This could be produced by forgetting to seal a newly constructed concrete-lined waterfall, for example; or lime or fresh concrete accidentally dropped into the pool. Other possible causes of lowered standard of health are overcrowding, rapid changes of water temperature, lowered oxygen content, and mild poisoning of the water.

Tail Rot

This disease attacks the fins and tails of fish, causing them to

88

rot away. It is produced by bacterial attack, but is unlikely to be contagious. Unfortunately there is seldom any effective cure and the affected fish is usually best removed and destroyed. The same sort of treatment as for fungus attack can be tried to arrest the disease, although even if successful the damaged parts of the fins and tail will not heal.

Wounds

Should a fish be injured in any way the wound will be very slow to heal naturally and will be open to fungus attack. The parasites causing fungus attack are normally present in any pool, but are innocuous as far as healthy fish are concerned. The rate of growth of fungus on a wounded fish, however, can be rapid.

The most effective treatment for an injured fish is to lift it gently from the pool on a damp cloth and gently dab the wounded area with a swab of cotton wool dipped in tincture of iodine. The wound should then be covered with a smear of Vaseline when the fish can be returned to the pool, or better still isolated in a 'hospital tank' until recovered.

White Spot

This is another disease caused by parasites, causing white lumps to appear on the body. It is contagious and affected fish should be removed for attention. This involves 'two-tank' treatment again, only this time a proprietary 'White spot' solution should be used instead of salt water. Exact concentration to be used and duration of treatment will be specified with the preparation.

The contagious effect of 'White spot' actually arises from the parasites causing the disease laying eggs which develop into free-swimming larvae which can attach themselves to other fish and so spread the disease. The life of these larvae in the free-swimming stage is only a matter of three days. Thus if a pond is affected, a complete cure can be brought about by removing all the fish for at least three days (and preferably a week). After that, all the larvae will have died and the fish can be returned to the pool with no fear of the disease spreading.

'White spot' is actually comparatively rare in garden pools. It is often confused with the initial stages of fungus disease.

Skin Eruptions

Holes in the skin, boils and other skin eruptions on the body of a fish may be caused by wormlike parasites which attach themselves to the body. Apart from causing 'localised' damage to individual fish such parasites are not particularly harmful unless they develop in large numbers in the pool.

Individual fish can be treated by removing from the pool and given the 'two-tank' treatment. The wormlike parasites may be clearly visible on the body of the fish, and can be removed with tweezers. Alternatively the attack may be by small lice, when the same treatment applies.

Where a pool becomes badly affected by worm parasites or fish lice it may be necessary to remove all the fish (whether affected or not) and sterilise the pool by adding several cupfuls of potash and salt. This should be left in the pool for several days, during which time all the parasites and their eggs will have been killed off. Before fish can be returned to the pool it will have to be pumped dry, refilled with fresh water and left to stand for a while, then pumped dry and filled again with fresh water. Alternatively it may be preferable to empty and clean out the pool completely, fill with water which is then sterilised as above, drain and wash and then refill and replant before the fish are re-introduced.

Cataract

Cataract is caused by the eye of a fish becoming infected with tiny worms which multiply rapidly and eventually cover the eye with a film of white. This is followed by the eye swelling and bulging as liquid gathers under the cornea. There is no positive cure for this disease, although a 'bath' treatment in potassium anti-monyl tartrate at a concentration of 1 grain per gallon can be effective in arresting the attack, if applied at a fairly early stage.

There are various other diseases fish may develop—tuberculosis, dropsy and exophthalamus ('bulging eye'), for example. Treatment will call for specialist advice, and will probably be more expensive than the value of the fish. Also success with treatment is generally limited. Any diseased fish represents a threat to the other inhabitants of the pool, so should be removed at once. The more kind-hearted will keep a 'hospital tank' ready for such emergencies; but the main requirement in such cases is to keep a close check on the pool itself to see that the disease is not spreading to other fish.

Breeding

In an established pool with a good natural balance and an abundance of oxygenating plants and other growth providing shade and shelter, breeding will occur naturally. A female, swollen with eggs in the spring, may be seen attended and apparently harassed by a male or two—which is quite a natural occurrence, the fish are not fighting. The process of nature can, in fact, be left to look after itself.

In due course the baby fish or 'fry' will appear, so tiny as to be virtually invisible. They will tend to collect in the areas of denser growth and shelter near the surface and it may be several weeks before they are large enough to be observed properly. Meantime the mortality rate amongst the fry will be quite high, but this is just as well. If not, a pool could become hopelessly overcrowded in a single season. As it is, in a properly established pool, its population may well double in the first year, yielding a number of inch-long youngsters to face the second season, reflecting their mixed parentage and ancestry by their colours and markings.

Where controlled breeding is the aim, a separate pond should be constructed and established for breeding, and stocked only with breeding pairs of a particular species. Adult fish are left to winter in this pool. After breeding in the later spring or early summer they can be removed to the main pool as soon as the fry appear, or can be left in the breeding pool if preferred. Small fish can be left to winter in their home pool, but are best removed and transferred to the main pool next spring before the next lot of fry are produced by their parents, as they are likely to exhibit cannibalistic habits towards their younger brothers and sisters. After maturing for several years in the main pool, they, too, can then be selected and paired off for breeding.

Isolating a breeding pair, or even two or three pairs, in a separate pool is about the only way of maintaining any control over the development of the fry. In the spring, the female should be observed regularly, to determine the time when she is driven in to the thicker weed area by the attendant male, where she will lay her eggs in the form of spawn adhering to the plants. These will then be fertilised by the male.

It will then normally take from about four to seven days for the fry to hatch out, depending on the water temperature; and it is well to remove all adults from the pool before the fry actually appear. They can then develop without the usual risk of being taken for food by larger fish, as will inevitably happen if they are left under natural conditions. Provided the breeding pool is well established there will be enough food present to support the fry, but additional feeding can be done with special fry food.

An alternative method which can be adopted is to wait until the eggs have been laid and fertilised, and then remove them to a separate empty pool or tank before the fry have hatched out. This can be done by lifting out the whole batch of plants to which the eggs are attached. Here it is necessary to distinguish between fish eggs and those laid by water snails. The latter are usually in the form of jelly-like ribbons, attached to the underside of floating leaves.

With this second method of treatment, the second tank or pool need only be prepared a week or so in advance of expected spawning, or even when required using 'conditioned' water drawn from a main pond. Feeding of the fry is then essential for their survival.

Remember, too, that the chances of successful breeding, whether under natural or 'controlled' conditions, depends on the adult pairs being in good health. That is why feeding the adult fish, even in a well-established pool, is generally recommended in the early spring months. Both ordinary and 'tonic' foods can be given, the latter including live chopped worms.

Breeding fish in any serious manner is, in fact, a complete subject on its own. There are a number of books written on this special subject which are worth consulting for more detailed information.

10

Care of the Pool

The properly stocked pool will more or less look after itself, although it may need some attention from time to time. It is quite usual, for example, for the water level to fall considerably during dry spells, and particularly so when the above water plant growth is at its most luxurious. The natural balance of water lost through evaporation being replaced by rain has been upset, and compensating for this by topping up with fresh water can do nothing but good. Natural balance can also be affected in other ways, particularly in small pools, as well as varying from season to season.

Cloudy or dirty looking water is usually the result of algae growth, which will tend to be most active in the lighter months of the year. Thus even in a properly balanced pond, water which is clear may well turn murky during early summer, because of an excess of algae.

Algae are, in fact, very simple forms of plant life, which turn up and multiply in practically all exposed waters, particularly static waters. They feed primarily on mineral salts contained in the water, and flourish in bright light, particularly sunlight. Logically, therefore, their control should be based on cutting down these two 'supplies'—e.g. with an abundance of oxygenating plants which also absorb mineral salts, and floating plants to provide shade for the water surface.

Even so it is often impossible to produce complete control of algae, although it should be possible to maintain clear water for most of the time, once the pool has become established and the plants properly settled in. This may take a month or so in a new pool, and there are no short-cut treatments. Changing the water, for example, will not make things better. It will simply start the process of algae development all over again. As a general rule, in fact, once a pool has been filled and planted the water should never be changed, unless something really drastic has gone wrong.

The green algae growth which collects on the pond sides, and perhaps on stones and pebbles in the shallower water, is less objectionable. It tends to produce a natural look to the pool, especially on the sides, and will normally be kept in check by water snails feeding off it. It is also beneficial to some extent, since it will give off oxygen and can thus be considered as part of the pool plant life which develops naturally.

The other type of algae which develops as masses of long, thin green threads, almost like cotton wool, can be objectionable, particularly as this can develop so rapidly at certain seasons. It is known variously as Blanket Weed, Flannel Weed, Silkweed, etc— and, in fact, there are various varieties. If allowed to develop to excess it can blanket and smother other plants, interfering with their proper development, and build up barriers which fish will find difficult to penetrate.

The simplest treatment when this occurs is to rake it out with the fingers, or a garden rake if the pool is a big one. Numerous small water snails may be found clinging to the slimy green mass, and these can be rubbed off and returned. Such a cure will only be temporary, for it is impossible to remove all the stringy algae in this way, and growth will start all over again, but at least it can be kept under control by regular 'weeding out'.

In very bad cases chemical treatment may be advised. As a general rule chemical treatment of pond waters is to be avoided, if possible, largely because the strength of chemicals necessary to be effective can be harmful to other life in the pool. However, there are certain proprietary chemicals made for algae control which are 'safe' and effective, *provided they are used at recommended strengths*. Instructions should be followed implicitly in this respect. Also dead algae resulting from treatment should be removed from the pool, not left to rot and sink.

An excess of decaying vegetation collecting at the bottom of the pool is the other main source of trouble. All plants will tend to die down in the winter, many shedding dead leaves. Leaves and other dead vegetation from the garden may well also fall into the pool, or be blown into it, to become waterlogged and sink. All this rubbish will eventually collect on the bottom and decompose, forming a layer of soil. This in itself is not harmful, except that the biological action of rotting consumes oxygen from the water, and gives off gases poisonous to fish (marsh gas or methane). The water itself may also become coloured to an inky blackness in fouled areas.

The naturally low oxygen content of pool water during the winter months emphasises the importance of including a number of oxygenating plants which do remain active during the winter amongst the plant collection.

Treatment here is to remove as much dead matter as possible from the pool as soon as it is formed, and whilst it is still floating and can readily be reached—e.g. using a child's shrimping net. The same treatment, incidentally, applies to grass cuttings which may be blown onto the surface of the pool during summer months. In a wooded garden it may well be expedient in autumn to cover the pool with a net to catch tree leaves and garden rubbish which would otherwise fall into the water—*Fig. 10.1*. A net covering during the winter months is also to be recommended in areas frequented by birds which are fish-feeders. Seagulls, for example, come inland for food during the winter months, whilst heron and similar waterside birds can clear a pool of fish in a single hour.

Winter is the worst time for the pool for the 'balance' of the pool is severely tested with the plants inactive, with the oxygen content of the water low. The fish compensate for this by their own inactivity and can, in fact, survive quite severe conditions—

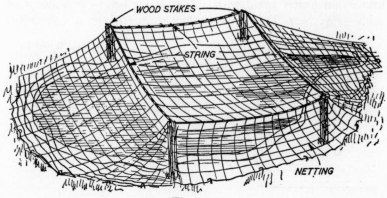

Fig. 10.1

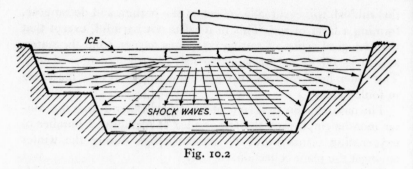

Fig. 10.2

even weeks of a pond being iced over, provided the bottom is not too foul with decomposing organic matter. To prevent too great a tax on their reserves, however, a pond should never be left iced over. Equally *never break up ice with sharp blows*. This will send severe shock waves through the water since water is incompressible and transfers a shock right through it—*Fig. 10.2*. This can stun fish, or even cause them internal damage.

The simplest way of making an opening in a pool which has iced over it to partly fill a bowl or jam jar with warm water and stand it on the ice. The heat will eventually melt the ice and form an opening, from which the bowl or jar can then be removed. This can be repeated at two or three points on the surface of the ice, if necessary.

Rather than such remedial treatment, *preventative treatment* is usually to be preferred, especially if the fish are valuable. This involves the use of a *pool heater* which is, basically, a simple immersion heater fitted with a float and a length of waterproof cable—*Fig. 10.3*. This cable is then connected to a convenient

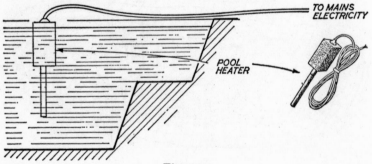

Fig. 10.3

source of mains electricity, so that it can be switched on when necessary. This could be done at night when a hard frost is forecast or the temperature is below freezing; or could be operated automatically off a thermostat.

The cable length supplied with pool heaters is generally fairly short. Since the nearest mains electricity point is likely to be several yards away and the cable is laid in 'wet' conditions, *the services of a qualified electrician should be sought when installing pool heaters*. They are not dangerous, nor can you get a shock by touching them, but in view of the fact that they are used in water with the cable running over damp ground, and exposed to rain, it is only commonsense to make sure that the complete installation is 'safe'.

A single pool heater will keep an area of about one foot diameter of the surface free from ice, even in the most severe weather. This will be adequate for most pools, although ideally, to keep the whole pond properly 'vented' to allow the escape of methane gas, one heater should be installed for every 25 to 30 square feet of surface area, spaced out accordingly.

Seasonal requirements for pool care are summarised in Table XIV. This is based on a pool with good 'balance'. Other things may go wrong, at any time, and need specific treatment.

The most common cause of trouble is oxygen deficiency, this being evidenced by the fish becoming sluggish and gulping air from the surface. Air gulping is almost always a symptom of oxygen deficiency.

The simplest treatment is to refresh the pool with a stream of fresh water directed from a hose and allowed to fall onto the surface—*Fig. 10.4*. This will carry down air into the water and

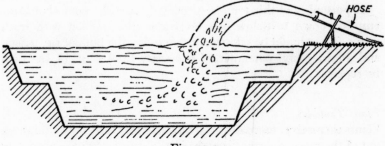

Fig. 10.4

introduce local circulation. Several areas of the pool can be treated in this manner. It does not matter if the pool is already full and overflows as a result.

In more drastic cases of oxygen starvation the water may be foul—and smell foul—and as well as showing distress, some fish may have died and are found floating on the surface. Unless a specific disease or cause can be determined—see Chapter 10— the best way of tackling this is to half empty the pool and refill with fresh water. This is where a fountain unit is valuable for it can be connected to work as a pump to pump out old water without sucking out fish, etc. Once pumped down to half level, or slightly lower, some of the rubbish can be cleared off the bottom—a messy, smelly business—and the pond refilled from a hose.

The *cause* of the trouble then wants looking for. Perhaps there are not enough oxygenating plants? Or has the bottom become thoroughly foul with decaying organic matter? Above all, do not be tempted to use chemical treatments for cure—other than for algae control if necessary. There is no substitute for a good natural balance, although the smaller the pool the more nature may have to be aided by 'adjusting' this balance from time to time.

Poisoned Water

Agricultural sprays, garden sprays, insecticides and weed killers can be regarded as poisons as far as garden pools are concerned. If allowed to get into the pool they can kill off the fish population, even in quite small concentrations. Thus, in general, no insecticide, insect killer of weed killer should be used near a garden pool, where there is any chance of it getting into the pool.

If poisoning of this type is suspected, then the pool should be emptied down to below half level and then refilled with fresh water. This should be effective in removing the bulk of the poison and diluting any remainder. If necessary the treatment can then be repeated.

Plant Troubles

Plants themselves normally need no particular care, only a thinning out of the more vigorous growths in the spring after the second or third season (and each spring thereafter), to prevent the pool becoming overcrowded with vegetation. Nor do they need any protection during the winter when they have died down and become dormant. Certain troubles and diseases may, however, show up from time to time.

Plant leaves may be attacked by larvae and other pests, often to the extent that they are skeletonised, or have large areas eaten away. This happens particularly in the case of plants with floating leaves. The larvae or insects can often be seen on the surface of the leaves, when an effective treatment is usually to wash them off with a hose fitted with a nozzle giving a fine spray.

In the event that a plant has become badly affected, however, it is best to remove it from the pool and immerse completely in a bucket containing derris solution for a few hours. The plant can then be removed, thoroughly washed under a tap or hose, and then replanted in the pool. Equally, if the plant is not a particularly useful or attractive one, it could be removed and thrown away, and replaced by an alternative if necessary.

Sometimes a plant crown will be attacked by red worms, causing it to rot and the leaves to decay. This is most likely to occur with water lilies, the symptoms being that the leaves turn brown with a curling of the edges. This can also occur when the plant is not happily settled in, or the conditions are not suitable— e.g. the depth of water is not right. A check is to pull gently on the stem of the leaf. If this is firm, the plant is just out of condition. If it comes away, the crown is probably infested with red worms. In this case the whole plant should be removed and soaked in derris solution, finally being washed before returning to the pool.

Pond plants should never be treated with insecticides—whether in the pool, or removed from it—as these are poisons as far as fish life in the pool is concerned. Also plants which are badly diseased should be removed and thrown away. Derris treatment should only be regarded as effective for attack by pests or early signs of disease. The 'pests' normally found in garden pools are, in fact, normally relatively harmless and are taken by many fish as food. Thus the fact that small red worms can be identified in the pool does not automatically apply that they will attack the crowns of water lilies. They will normally show a preference for feeding on decaying matter.

TABLE XIV SEASONAL CARE OF THE POOL

Month	Action
January	See that the surface is kept open for the pool to 'breathe' in the freezing weather.
February	As for January.
March	Protective netting can be removed. Plants can be thinned out, if necessary. Clean out bottom rubbish if necessary. Start feeding fish with 'tonic' foods, but do not overfeed.
April	Good time to build a new pool. Some plants ready for planting (see Chapter 7). Continue feeding fish.
May	New fish can be introduced, if required. New plants can be introduced, if required. First water lilies can be planted.
June	Carry on planting out and stocking a new pool. Remove stringy green algae as it builds up. Feeding the fish is no longer necessary in an established pool. Top up pool level regularly, if necessary. The first of the season's fry should now be large enough to be visible.
July	Keep on top of algae growth. Top up pool regularly and spray with water from a hose to assist aeration.
August	More stringy algae growth will need removing. No further planting should be attempted.
September	Start removing dead leaves from plants and keep water surface clean. Some weeding out of plants may also be necessary.
October	Clean pool bottom by removing dead, sunken leaves and other debris. Remove all decaying matter from the pool. Cover with netting to keep falling leaves off the water.

Month	Action
November	Water heater(s) should be placed in pool and connected up ready to combat freezing over. Net should be placed over pool to keep birds off (unless already fitted in October).
December	Make sure that water heaters are functioning properly or make holes in ice if the pool freezes over.

TABLE XV PLANT PESTS

Pest	Remarks
Midge larvae	May eat holes in leaves, even reducing them to skeleton form if attack is severe. Wash larvae off leaves into the pool, where they will be eaten by the fish.
Red worm (larvae)	Attacks leaves, particularly those of water lilies, and may also attack water lily crowns and roots. Affected plants can be removed for treatment with derris. An adequate number of fish will normally keep these pests under control.
Water beetles	Generally unharmful, but may eat leaves and attack water lily buds. Spray with water to wash off.
Greenfly	Attack and eat leaves and water lily buds. Spray with water to wash off. *Do not spray with insecticide.*
Miscellaneous insects	Generally unharmful, although they may attack leaves and plants locally. Wash off with a spray of water.

11

Pool Accessories

The most attractive accessories for any garden pool are undoubtedly a fountain and waterfall. These also form a functional as well as a decorative purpose by circulating the pond water which assists in raising its oxygen content and, just as important, maintaining a cooler water temperature in hot weather.

The one basic rule to be observed is that water for a fountain or waterfall, or both, should be drawn from the pool itself, so that it is only pool water which is being recirculated. If water is drawn from another source, this could upset the balance of the pool. A fountain and/or waterfall system, therefore, is normally based on a submersible pump fitted in the pool itself. This is a simple water pump driven by an electric motor enclosed in a waterproof housing and with a waterproof bearing and extension lead to connect to a mains electricity point. The pump can remain completely submerged indefinitely—although it would normally be advisable to remove it during the winter months to prevent possible ice damage to the impeller.

The actual pump is usually a simple centrifugal type with a plastic impeller. The inlet side is fitted with a simple strainer which prevents weed, etc., being drawn into the pump. The outlet is in the form of a straight tube, usually positioned vertically. To this can be attached an extension tube of suitable length, with a spray head to produce a fountain spray—see *Fig. 11.1*. Some form of adjustment is usually also incorporated either in the pump outlet tube, or in the tube leading to the fountain spray head. Alternatively heads are available giving different spray patterns— see *Fig. 11.2*. The actual strength of the spray can also be varied by the adjuster.

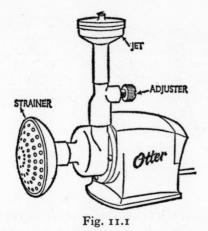

Fig. 11.1

If preferred, an external water pump can be used rather than a submersible type. In this case the pump is set up in a suitable enclosure by the side of the pool, drawing water from the pool through a suction line fitted with a strainer—*Fig. 11.3*. The pump outlet is then connected by a separate hose to the fountain or a fountain ornament mounted in the pool.

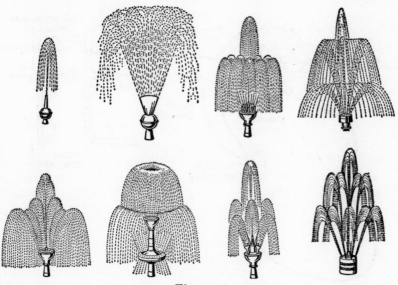

Fig. 11.2

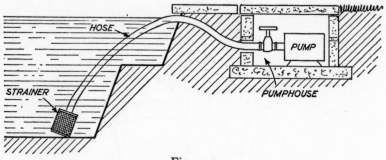

Fig. 11.3

With such a system it is usual to provide two or three branches on the pump outlet, either controlled by separate stopcocks or blanked off when not required. One outlet would be used for feeding a fountain, another for feeding a waterfall, and a third for emptying the pool when opened and the other two outlets turned off—see *Fig. 11.4*.

The only real advantages offered by this system are that the pump itself is readily accessible at all times and normally needs

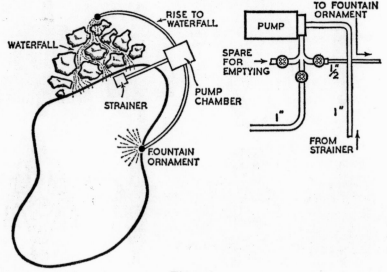

Fig. 11.4

only to be damp-proof rather than fully waterproof; and the mains electricity connected to the pump does not have to enter the pool water although it must still be a fully waterproof cable.

Fountains

The height to which the fountain spray is ejected depends on the 'head' which the pump will develop. This depends both on the size of pump and the amount of water it is pumping—see Table XVI. Thus reducing the output, e.g. by closing the adjuster to restrict the flow, a higher fountain spray can be produced, but with less water ejected through the spray. The actual height of spray will be rather less than that shown by the pump performance figures since there will be some loss of head due to friction through the delivery pipe, and particularly through the spray nozzle.

To work effectively the spray head must protrude above the surface of the water. If below it will simply pump water into the pool without generating a spray. The pump unit is thus supported on rocks laid on the bottom of the pool, built up to the correct height—see *Fig. 11.5*. The waterproof lead can be laid along the bottom of the pool and taken out at a convenient point where it can be hidden from view, and thence to a connecting point for the mains supply. The fountain will then operate as long as the pump motor supply is switched on.

A point to be watched when a high fountain spray is used in a relatively small pool is that part of the spray may well fall outside

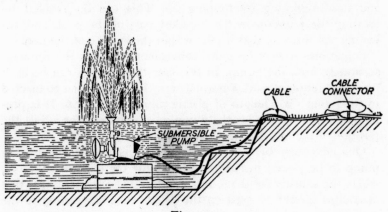

Fig. 11.5

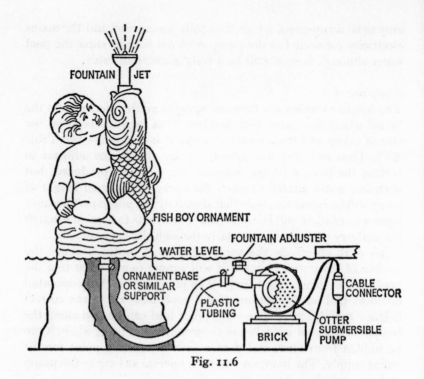

FOUNTAIN JET

FISH BOY ORNAMENT

FOUNTAIN ADJUSTER

WATER LEVEL

ORNAMENT BASE
OR SIMILAR
SUPPORT

PLASTIC
TUBING

CABLE
CONNECTOR

OTTER
SUBMERSIBLE
PUMP

BRICK

Fig. 11.6

the edges of the pool, particularly in windy weather. A proportion of pool water will therefore be lost when the fountain is operating and need replacing by topping up. This can be avoided by locating the fountain in the broadest part of the pool, and adjusting the spray so that it falls within the surface of the pool.

Sometimes it may be more convenient to locate the fountain separately from the pump. In this case the fountain can be built up where required, with a normal spray head, and then connected to the pump via a length of plastic tubing—*Fig. 11.6*. It is preferable in this case to lay the pump unit on its side, or adjust the position of the outlet pipe, to give horizontal delivery.

One advantage of this 'remote' set up is that it enables the pump to be placed in shallow water near the edge of the pool, where the adjuster for the fountain is readily accessible. Note that hose clips should be used on the plastic tube connecting to the pump outlet and fountain fitting.

Waterfalls

A submersible pump can also be used to work a waterfall. In this case a length of hose is taken from the pump delivery tube to the top of the waterfall—*Fig. 11.7*. This hose can be buried, except where it emerges from the pool over the edge, where it can be hidden with a stone slab. No adjuster is required in this case or if fitted should be fully open so that the full flow of the pump is achieved. The maximum height to which the hose can be carried is then rather less than the minimum head specified for the pump, allowing for frictional losses in the hose. A larger diameter hose should always be used—$\frac{3}{4}$ inch rather than the usual $\frac{1}{2}$ inch.

Fig. 11.7

The waterfall itself can be constructed from natural materials, such as rocks, with a suitable waterway passage, made to look as natural as possible. The main problem then lies in waterproofing this waterway, so that all the water pumped to the top is returned to the pool instead of a proportion seeping away through the rocks. In fact, this can prove quite difficult. Concrete can be used to seal the gaps, but will need a waterproofing treatment (see Chapter 5). Also it will be very likely to crack and develop leaks. For this

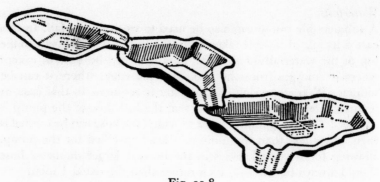

Fig. 11.8

reason many people will prefer to use small prefabricated rigid mouldings, available in various shapes. These can be used singly or together to form cascades, streams and waterfalls, the pool sections having special pouring lips—e.g. see *Fig. 11.8*. Besides offering considerable flexibility in layout, such assemblies can be made to look quite natural by arranging natural rocks around them —this also serving to hold them in place.

No attempt should be made to plant cascade pools as the running water will only wash the soil away; nor should fish be introduced in them.

Combined Fountain and Waterfall
The same pump can be used to provide both a fountain and waterfall. In this case the outlet pipe is tapped with a tee, providing two outfeeds—*Fig. 11.9*. One is connected by hose to the top of the waterfall; and the other fitted directly with a fountain tube and

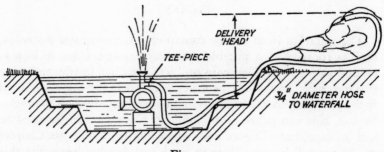

Fig. 11.9

spray head, or connected by hose to a remote fountain. Because the pump is now producing two separate supplies the head available at the fountain and waterfall will be approximately halved. This must be allowed for in deciding a suitable height for the waterfall, although the head available on the waterfall hose can always be increased by cutting down the fountain supply via the adjuster.

Low or High Voltage

The majority of submersible pumps developed for garden pool use are designed to operate on mains voltage (240–250 volts AC). This represents no particular hazard, provided they are properly and efficiently connected to the supply. However, for those people who dislike the thought of using mains electricity 'outdoors' it is possible to find small water pumps which will operate off 12 volts. In this case they can either be worked off a car battery (which could be installed in a nearby garden shed), or from mains electricity via a 12-volt transformer. In the latter case only the low voltage (12 volt) supply cable need be 'outside'. All mains connections, including the transformer, can be inside the house.

Suitable types of small pumps for low voltage working are those produced primarily, or specifically, as bilge pumps for small boats, when they are designed to work off a 12-volt battery (or in some cases a 24-volt battery). Some have fully sealed motor units and may be regarded as fully immersible, but the majority are not intended to operate with the water level above the lower bearing of the motor. If such pumps are used, therefore, they should be installed in a separate 'pumphouse' external to the pool, as in *Fig. 11.3*. Some difficulty may, however, be experienced in arranging a suitable suction feed, for the majority of bilge pumps are designed to 'stand' in a few inches of water and suck up water directly throught their base unit. This would have to be adapted to take a suction pipe to lead into the pool. In general, too, they will not suck as well as an immersible pump, unless installed in a 'wet' sump with a water level of a few inches.

Connecting to Mains Electricity Supply

The length of waterproof lead supplied ready-connected to the pump will seldom be long enough to reach to the nearest electricity point (10 feet cable length is more or less standard, although some pumps may have a longer cable). It must, therefore, be connected to a further length of 3-core cable, using a *waterproof cable connector*, to reach back to the nearest 3-pin electricity socket. The connector itself should be protected from rain by covering with paving slabs.

If in doubt, call in the help of a qualified electrician to ensure that the installation is completely safe and represents no hazard. A badly placed connecting cable could, for example, be accidentally cut by a lawnmower, or when digging the garden, which could be dangerous if it was switched on and 'live'. Properly installed, there is no more danger in carrying mains electricity supply to a pool than in any other mains electricity installation.

Pool Lighting

Since a pool is normally constructed as a feature of the garden, further interest can be achieved by providing illumination at night. Two types of lighting can be considered—one using simple spotlights mounted above ground, and the other submerged lights in the pool itself. Both types can, of course, be combined in a single display.

In either case *only special lamps made for the purpose should be used*. These are fully sealed and double insulated throughout. Once again such lamps are most commonly designed for mains voltage operation, but low voltage lamps are also available. These are intended to operate off a 12-volt transformer, but could also be battery operated. A mains supply via a transformer is more reliable, especially if more than one lamp is used. Lamps are invariably connected in parallel, and with several lamps in circuit the current drain will be too high to be met satisfactorily by a car battery.

Above ground lamps are usually mounted on a spike attached to the lamp body. The spike is pushed into the ground to 'base' level, and the lamp position adjusted by turning or angling on its top pivot—see *Fig. 11.10*.

Underwater lamps are normally mounted on a flat based stand and stood in the pool, supported by rocks placed on the base. Again the lamps can readily be adjusted for angle.

An alternative type of lamp is the floating light, so constructed that it is fully buoyant. One or more of these lamps can be suitably anchored by their connecting cable to provide general lighting;

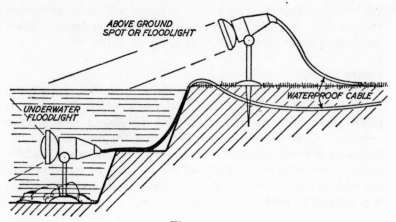

Fig. 11.10

or can be weighted down to provide submerged lighting—*Fig. 11.11*.

Once again the importance of only using lamps specifically designed for the purpose must be emphasised. Underwater lamps must obviously be fully waterproof. Above ground lamps still need to be waterproof, and must be unaffected by condensation or rain falling on them. A common construction is, in fact, normally used for both types—so that an individual lamp can be used either above ground or submerged—with both 'flood' and 'spot' reflectors, and with various coloured glasses. A flood lamp would be chosen for underwater illumination. Either a flood or a spot, or combinations of both, could be used above ground, according to the pattern of illumination required. Matching cable units are

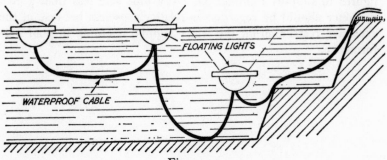

Fig. 11.11

available for connecting up a series of lamps with fully waterproof connections, but the same general recommendations about connecting to the mains electricity apply as above.

Filters

Where a pump is used for a fountain or waterfall, a filter can be inserted in the pump curcuit through which the water is passed and solid contaminants removed. This is not usual practice —in fact, most authorities will hold that filtering is quite unnecessary in a well-balanced pool. Nevertheless, filters are available specially designed for garden pool use and may be found of considerable assistance in keeping pool water clean and clear where it is difficult to establish a natural balance.

Pond and Garden Ornaments

Many specialist suppliers concentrate on producing a range of garden ornaments which are suitable accessories for garden pools— for example, fountains in various figure and animal shapes and sculpted features. Some people feel that ornamentation adds a lot to the beauty and attraction of a garden pool; others prefer that the pool should maintain a natural appearance. It is purely a matter of personal preference. There is no need to describe such ornaments in detail here since they are illustrated and described in the catalogues of the various manufacturers. It may be mentioned, however, that the quality available can vary enormously, from inexpensive plaster figures to those sculpted in natural stone, or cast in bronze or lead (the latter being for decorative figures only, not working fountains).

There is a great deal of variety in the pipework sizes used in figures to support fountain jets. Any pipe size less than $\frac{1}{2}$ inch diameter should be regarded as relatively useless because of the excessive restriction on the water supply, resulting in poor performance.

TABLE XVI PERFORMANCE TABLE FOR SUBMERSIBLE PUMPS

Pump	Output in gallons per hour, at a head of :						Shut off (max. head)	Watts
	3 ft.	5 ft.	7 ft.	10 ft.	14 ft.	20 ft.		
Otter	330	240	120	–	–	–	8 ft.	90
Little Giant	500	400	350	260	100	–	16 ft.	110
Sealion 'A'	1300	1000	600	–	–	–	10 ft.	200
Sealion 'C'	2000	1900	1750	1550	1250	700	26 ft.	300
Big John	3000	2500	2100	1400	600	–	16 ft.	350

TABLE XVIA CAPACITIES AND HEAD OF TYPICAL SURFACE PUMPS

Make	Model	Output in gallons per hour at a head of:								Max. suct. lift	Max. watts	H.P.	Type of motor	Dimensions Length × Height
		5 ft.	10 ft.	15 ft.	20 ft.	25 ft.	30 ft.	35 ft.	40 ft.					
Stuart	No. 12	600	540	480	420	360	300	200		15 ft.	200	1/9	Series	10½ in. × 5¾ in.
Wade	Mini	750	625	450	250					5 ft.	115	1/8	Induc.	9½ in. × 5½ in.
Stuart	No. 18	720	600	400						8 ft.	170	1/6	Induc.	12⅛ in. × 6½ in.
Beresford	PV.100	3200	3020	2700	2240	1680	800			23 ft.	750	3/4	Induc.	14½ in. × 7 in.
Stuart	No. 25	1000	950	900	850	800	700	500		15 ft.	550	1/2	Induc.	12¾ in. × 7¼ in.
*Wade	DC./2S	1800	1760	1700	1670	1560	1420	1270	1120	15 ft.	750	3/4	Induc.	13 in. × 7½ in.
†Wade	RC./2	2100	2000	1980	1950	1860	1825	1800		15 ft.	950	1	Induc.	13½ in. × 8⅝ in.

* Output in gallons per hour at a head of: at 45 ft. 920 g.p.h.; at 50 ft. 660 g.p.h.

† Output in gallons per hour at a head of: at 50 ft. 1680 g.p.h.; at 60 ft. 1320 g.p.h.; at 70 ft. 840 g.p.h.

The expression 'head' refers to the vertical distance between the pool water surface level and the outlet; in water garden use, the head is normally relatively low. However, pressure losses in pipework and fittings increase the actual head against which the pump is working. The outputs shown against a head of 5 ft. are the maximum outputs of which the pumps are capable, and must not be exceeded, though they can be reduced to any desired level by stopcock adjustment. At such reduced outputs, current consumption is also reduced.